The Road to Hell

How purposeful business leads to bad
marketing and a worse world*

* And how human creativity is the way out

First published in the United Kingdom in 2024 by
The Choir Press

ISBN 978-1-78963-448-8

For Dad, who walked with a purpose

Contents

THE ROAD TO HELL

Prologue

IN EARLY 2010, I was pondering a single word in a document on my screen, cursor blinking.

I'm a writer whose day job involves helping brands communicate what they do, using creative language and ideas. In this case, I was working for a branding agency, whose client was one of the big four global management consultancies.

The document was a business pitch that the management consultancy was preparing: a narrative that they would use to attract business from corporate clients around the world. This was a big deal for them, and my job was to edit and inject some life into the existing copy.

So far, I liked it. The pitch told a story of how business had fallen out of favour since the financial crisis of 2007–2008, when Lehman Brothers went under and $2 trillion was wiped off the global economy. The pitch talked honestly about the failings of big business, acknowledging that the reputation of global corporations was at a perilous low. The challenge now was to rehabilitate the reputation of business, by reminding people of the good things it did for society. Businesses employ people. They innovate, generate wealth and pay taxes. Sometimes a single business can sustain a whole community or town. The limited company is a clever invention that enables innovation to happen, with all the good effects that come from it.

I liked where this was going. It felt like an honest

acknowledgement of corporate and regulatory failings, and a useful corrective to some of the anti-business overreach in the public reaction. We need to remind people of how useful business is, said the pitch. We need to remind people that business can contribute positively to society, continued the pitch. We need to remind people of the *purpose* of business…

We're all prone to post-rationalise, but I distinctly remember this moment, as I pondered the 'purpose' word.

So far, the tone of the pitch had been refreshingly grounded. The argument about reminding people of the upsides of business was credible and persuasive. But to say this was the *purpose* of business? That felt like a whole other claim.

It's one thing to say business can make a useful societal contribution. It's another thing to say this is the purpose that gets executives out of bed every morning and steers the big decisions in the boardroom, or the micro-decisions in the workplace. The pitch had started out by acknowledging the hubris that led to 2008. But now it was straying into a different kind of hubris: making a moral claim about the fundamental motivation of corporations.

The cursor blinked at the p-word and I did the same. Scanning forward in the text, I noted that 'purpose' was the central theme in the remaining sections, and the key thought binding the whole story together. Rewriting it would be complicated and no doubt not welcomed by the client.

I had bills to pay and other work to do.

I still wish I'd pressed delete.

Introduction

8 OCTOBER 2008. The United Kingdom is hours away from a "breakdown of law and order" as the Labour chancellor Alistair Darling would later describe it. The Chief Executive of the Royal Bank of Scotland Group has stepped down and the government has stepped in with £50 billion of public money to save the banking sector.

25 JULY 2023. The Chief Executive of Coutts, part of the NatWest Group, formerly known as the Royal Bank of Scotland Group, has stepped down following a row about the withdrawal of banking services from former Brexit Party leader Nigel Farage. The decision comes after an internal report detailing how Farage no longer aligned with the 'values' of the bank. The bank is still nearly 40% owned by the UK taxpayer.

***

10 NOVEMBER 2010. Parliament Square in London is packed with 50,000 students protesting the trebling of tuition fees by the Conservative / Liberal Democrat coalition government, despite an electoral pledge by the Liberal Democrats to oppose such an increase. Lib Dem leader Nick Clegg will later apologise for the u-turn, which heralds a decade of austerity politics.

14 MARCH 2022. The former Head of Strategy for the 2010 Liberal Democrat election campaign, and Director of Policy from 2010 to 2015, takes on a newly created position at University of the Arts London. Her mission is to lead a rising generation of politically aware students who see 'art as a form of activism'. Her title is Chief Social Purpose Officer.[1]

***

17 SEPTEMBER 2011. Wall Street is packed with protestors angry about economic inequality, corporate greed and the influence of money in politics—a protest sparked by the editors of anti-consumerist publication Adbusters and publicised with an image of a dancer atop the iconic bull sculpture.

8 MARCH 2017. The protestors have disappeared from Wall Street. In their place is a bronze statue of a girl facing down the bull. Fearless Girl is the brain child of ad agency McCann and asset management firm State Street, who will later be sued by their female employees for systemic pay inequality, and by the female sculptor for curtailing her creative expression. The idea is hailed by the global ad industry and becomes one of the most awarded campaigns in Cannes history.

***

This book is about what happened in between.
It's about a single word: purpose.

Some readers will be unaware of the special meaning that gathered round this word in the marketing and business world over the course of the 2010s. Maybe you noticed how ads became more earnest over that period: more saving the world, fewer laughs or catchy jingles. Maybe you noticed business leaders becoming more vocal about social issues. If you're in the UK, you might remember a culture war skirmish, in which Conservative minister Kemi Badenoch criticised the political stance of Ben and Jerry's. If you're in the US, you might recall the Battle of Bud Light or the cat-and-mouse fights between DeSantis and the Disney Corporation. Wherever you are in the world, you can't fail to have noticed the rise of trillion-dollar companies, celebrity oligarchs and a widening wealth gap.

Other readers will be more attuned to the marketing and business world debate, and already tired of it. Those readers will be aware that the word 'purpose' has been at the centre of a tangled debate about the social role of businesses, and how that affects their marketing. Some may have arrived at the conclusion that purpose is all in the nuance. Sure, there are charlatans and hypocrites who talk a good purpose game to conceal what's really happening. But it shouldn't put us off the real thing: purpose is good when it's real, bad when it isn't. End of book.

That would be an easy book to write, and many have written it.

This is a harder book to write, and no one else has written it in the way I'd like. I'll be making the case that purpose—even, or especially, when it's 'real'—is an incoherent way to think about marketing, business and business ethics.

The clue to my argument is in the title of the book.

It comes from an English proverb: 'The road to hell is paved with good intentions'. And my argument is that, for all the (sometimes) good intentions behind purpose, it's a fundamentally flawed concept that leads to bad marketing and worse outcomes for society.

I'll make that argument by talking about what purpose is, where it came from, how it leads to worse marketing, and how it leads to a worse world. Then I'll make a positive case for an alternative, based on a combination of creativity, cognitive empathy, and valuing the human over the corporate.

All this matters because, even if you are tired of the purpose debate, you can't afford to be tired of what it's fundamentally about: the role of business in society, and the political and ethical dimensions of what businesses and marketers do every day.

For over a decade, purpose has warped clear thinking around that question, to the point where things have happened that would have seemed inconceivable to the Wall Street protestors in 2011, the student protestors in 2010, and the public watching in 2008 as £50 billion of their money disappeared into the ether.

First, we'd better start with some definitions.

1.
What is purpose?

We're not here because we're free. We're here because we're not free. There's no escaping reason, no denying purpose. Because, we both know, without purpose, we would not exist. It is purpose that created us, purpose that connects us, purpose that pulls us, that guides us, that drives us. It is purpose that defines us, purpose that binds us.

– Agent Smith, *The Matrix*, shortly before multiple
Agent Smiths attack a confused Neo

WHEN IT COMES TO purpose, starting with definitions is more than just throat-clearing. It gets you pretty rapidly into the heart of the debate.

Some readers may be puzzled by this whole question. What's wrong with purpose? Isn't purpose a good and necessary thing? Especially the kind of moral purpose that drives human lives? Isn't it important to consider whether existence has a purpose? Haven't philosophers pondered such questions for centuries?

Yes—these are questions to which we'll return. Purpose is a deep and meaningful concept. It's a word that existed long before it was co-opted by the business and marketing world, and it will continue to exist long afterwards.

For now, I want to start with the special meaning that the word 'purpose' has accumulated over the last two decades. And it's important to make sure I'm grappling with the same definition as the one used by the most influential people on the purpose side of the debate, because otherwise we're doomed to talk past each other. Purpose advocates will hopefully be with me as I set out this definition.

Five pillars of purpose

In the business and marketing context, I suggest there are five pillars to the definition of purpose.

1. Purpose is distinct from profit

"Purpose is the reason a business exists beyond making money." Jim Stengel, author of Grow: How Ideals Power Growth and Profit at the World's Greatest Companies (2011)

"The brands that will thrive in the coming years are the ones that have a purpose beyond profit." Richard Branson, founder of the Virgin Group (2014)

On the pro-purpose side, purpose is defined as a concept distinct from profit. The argument is that the two can be aligned, but it rests on the recognition that there is a tension to be resolved. According to the mantra of the purpose movement, businesses should 'Do well by doing good'. The 'do well' part is making a profit; the 'do good' part is making a positive social impact. The argument is about how they relate.

At this point, it's worth distinguishing humdrum, lower-case, pre-2008 'purpose' from the special, upper-case Purpose that replaced it. Before 2008, by a conventional reading, the lower-case purpose of a business was to make a profit. Or if you wanted to get more granular about it, the purpose of a particular business was to sell widgets that make a profit. Those widgets might have the benefit of making life easier for people who need widgets—indeed, it would be hard to sell them otherwise. But in order to steer its course, the business need focus only on the profit motive. As long as the widgets are selling, everyone's happy.

Capital-P Purpose is a bigger idea than that. It's the idea

that businesses need a higher reason to exist: something that goes beyond the act of selling whatever it is they sell to generate a profit. This was the distinct meaning that purpose took on around 2008: the idea of an outward-looking purpose that went beyond the core profit-making activities and sought to make the world a better place.

2. Purpose is about the why

"People don't buy what you do; they buy why you do it." Simon Sinek, author of Start With Why (2009)

"Purpose, or an organization's 'why,' is the fundamental reason why you do what you do as a company." Sara Roberts, Executive Director in the Advisory Services practice, Ernst & Young (2017)

Related to this, purpose is frequently connected to the question 'why'.

Naturally enough, companies usually talk about *what* they sell, the times in life *when* you might need it, *how* it might make your life easier, *where* it comes from or *where* it's on sale, *who* makes it or *who* it's aimed at.

The question 'why', according to purpose advocates, takes you somewhere deeper. It's about the fundamental motivation that drives what you do. According to Simon Sinek's influential 2009 TED talk, the 'how' and 'what' always emerge from this primal 'why'. As he puts it, Apple believes in "thinking differently and challenging the status quo in everything they do [why]. They do this by creating beautifully designed products that are a joy to use and a pleasure to own [how]." Then Sinek finishes with a nonchalant shrug: "They just happen to sell computers [what]."

We'll come back to this.

3. Purpose has a moral and social valence

"Society is demanding that companies, both public and private, serve a social purpose." Larry Fink, CEO, BlackRock (2018)

"In order for any brand to be purposeful, it must advocate for a high-order ideal and put itself in service to people and the world. So, by definition, every purpose-driven brand yields social or societal benefits." Jim Stengel

An essential characteristic of purpose is that it carries a moral and social valence. If the 'why' of a company is simply to make widgets, there's little point in introducing the purpose word in the first place—you can simply stick to the conventional profit motive. Purpose goes beyond that. When used by powerful players such as Larry Fink, CEO of BlackRock, or when it's the title of newly introduced categories in global advertising awards, or when it's the subject of press articles and hotly contested debates about the role of business in society, purpose is synonymous with the idea of 'social purpose'. For Jim Stengel, author of Grow (2011), purpose is about 'high-order ideals' that yield 'social or societal benefits'.

Crucially, this is what made purpose feel new and different as it rose to prominence post-2008. Without that moral and social valence, it would be an idea no different to the missions, strategies, propositions and brand ideas that companies had been talking about for decades.

4. Purpose is deeper than marketing

"I really cringe at the idea of companies using purpose as 'positioning' or as a marketing gimmick. It's truly inauthentic—and most times you can tell when they are trying to talk the talk but really don't walk the walk. To quote Lady Gaga, I think the truly authentic companies were 'born that way'. They came up from this desire to be a force for good in the world, along with making money." Sara Roberts, Ernst & Young[2]

"Talking is not enough. It is critical that brands take action and demonstrate their commitment to making a difference." Alan Jope, CEO of Unilever, 2019-2023

This is a recurring point in any pro-purpose argument: it only works when it's authentic. It needs to be business-deep. It's not just a feel-good story you tell in order to make your brand feel topical or worthy. It's not just superficial 'purpose-washing' that you do to burnish your image. It has to come from a systemic and demonstrable commitment to a cause. It's a business idea, not a branding idea.

I sign up to this part of the definition. It's what makes

purpose so consequential as a concept. More than just a marketing fad, it's a way for businesses to conceptualise their place in the world and the ethical responsibilities that flow from it.

5. Purpose is your reason for being

"Purpose is not a mere tagline or marketing campaign; it is a company's fundamental reason for being." Larry Fink, CEO, BlackRock

"In a survey conducted by EY Beacon Institute and Harvard Business Review Analytic Services, 90% of executives said their companies now recognize the importance of having 'an aspirational reason for being which inspires and provides a call to action for an organization... and provides benefit to society'." Valerie Keller and Caroline Webb, Harvard Business Review, 2017.

Finally, purpose is commonly cited as a company's 'reason for being'. It's the answer to the question: 'What are we for?'

Larry Fink defined it this way in his influential letter in 2019, one of a series of annual open letters that he addresses to the people who steer the multinationals who steer the brands who appoint the agencies who create the advertising campaigns. These CEOs naturally pay attention to one of the largest asset management firms on the planet, controlling up to $10 trillion in money that flows through public companies and influences their decision-making. If Larry Fink says a company must have a social purpose, it's in the self-interest of CEOs to agree.

***

So hopefully we're broadly agreed on the definition. Purpose is a social purpose that is distinct from the commercial motive; it's about a company's 'why'; it has a moral and social valence that elevates it above conventional business language; it's a business-deep idea, not just a marketing idea; and it defines an organisation's fundamental reason for being.

This is the concept of purpose that this book is arguing against—and it will take the whole book to do it. For now, I want to plant a flag on that last 'reason for being' phrase.

In the English language, we have long-standing terminology that defines the 'reason for being' of an organisation—an answer to the question: 'What is the organisation *for*?'.

From the first moment of their creation, we define some organisations as *for*-profits.

And others as not-*for*-profits.

A lot hinges on this terminology. As a society, we've always treated the distinction as meaningful. We tax these organisations differently, and have different expectations of them. We expect not-for-profits to intervene in social issues, because that is their reason for being. Indeed, we feel more comfortable about it because we know they're *not* doing it for profit.

In theory, a for-profit organisation could take public

donations to send food to starving children, deliver a greater impact-per-dollar through superior efficiencies, and cream off the rest in dividends to shareholders. If the social impact is greater than whatever the charities are managing to deliver, it shouldn't bother us. But it does. It just feels icky for companies to make a profit from certain activities, even if they perform well in the starving children market. Instead, we give that social licence to not-for-profits, knowing that, once operating costs are covered, all the money will be reinvested in the cause.

Traditionally, we haven't expected for-profit companies to claim the same authority to intervene in social issues. They are limited companies partly in the sense of being limited in the scope of their social licence and authority. As a society, we agree to give business owners the unusual and liberating gift of limited liability, on the basis that they limit their activities to their core business.

That social contract is called into question by corporate purpose. While framed as a noble attempt to 'step up' and tackle issues beyond the conventional realm of business, it can also be seen as a concerted attempt to step *into* realms that are beyond the remit of limited companies—operating, as they must, in a compromising web of market forces.

We'll explore this argument at more length later.

First, there's another way to define purpose, which is to look it up in the dictionary.

Two kinds of purpose

Let's go with the Oxford Languages definition that you'll see when you Google it.

purpose (noun)

1. the reason for which something is done or created or for which something exists. "the **purpose** of the meeting is to appoint a trustee"

Similar: motive, motivation, grounds, cause, impetus, occasion, reason, point, basis, justification, intention, aim, object, objective, goal, end, plan, scheme, target, ambition, aspiration, desire, wish, hope, advantage, benefit, good, use, usefulness, value, merit, worth, gain, profit, avail, result, outcome, effect, mileage, percentage, behoof, boot, function, role, raison d'être

2. a person's sense of resolve or determination. "there was a new **sense of purpose** in her step as she set off"

Similar: determination, resoluteness, resolution, resolve, firmness (of purpose), steadfastness, backbone, drive, push, thrust, enthusiasm, ambition, initiative, enterprise, motivation, single-mindedness, commitment, conviction, dedication, get-up-and-go

You can see how the primary definition is the same as Larry Fink's 'reason for being'. Indeed, the list of similar words ends with 'raison d'être', which is how a French Larry Fink might put it. (The list also includes the word 'profit', which feels like Oxford Languages is trying to make a point.)

But the secondary meaning is a clue to why purpose has been such a powerful concept in recent years. While it's used mainly in the primary sense of 'reason for being', it also comes with strong, positively-valenced overtones of conviction, determination, backbone and resolve. Even for those who claim they mean 'purpose' in a more pragmatic and commercial sense, the word still carries these moral overtones. Purpose is a puff-your-chest-out word: a word that sounds deeper and more noble than 'proposition' or 'target' or 'goal'. And it's clear that many purpose advocates use the word 'purpose' at least partially in this secondary sense—to express an attitude and state of mind. By that reading, 'purpose' isn't necessarily a categorical claim about a business's reason for being. It's more a statement of intent: a deeply held resolve to do good.

This nuance will recur throughout the book. But for now, let's note two things. Firstly, when it comes to organising large groups of people into complex systems like corporations and markets, incentives play a greater role than intentions. You can intend great outcomes all you like, but intention alone won't change the countless micro-incentives that affect each decision made at every level of the system. Indeed, your strongly held intentions may end up blinding you to the subtler incentives that are shaping what you do. The road

THE ROAD TO HELL

to hell is paved with good *purposes* in that secondary sense.

But there is also a philosophical question about whether a business can even have a purpose in the secondary 'state of mind' sense. In the end, a business is a legal construct, not possessed of a conscience or inner sense of resolve. The only way purpose can exist in the secondary sense is in people.

It will become clear, especially towards the end of the book, that this is a crucial distinction. For all that I'm a sceptic of business purpose, I'm not against the idea of human purpose. If anything, I see it as the essential counterbalance to the logical momentum of corporations.

So we've defined this term that, I argue, will ultimately lead us to hell.

Now, where the hell did it come from?

2.
Where did purpose come from?

Man plans, God laughs.

– Yiddish proverb

HERE COMES THE HISTORY bit. It's a light skip through centuries of backstory, but it's important because every part of it illuminates the present. Fundamentally, purpose is a reframing of a conversation that is as old as business itself.

And that is pretty old.

Japan to Jerusalem

Founded in 578 AD, Japanese construction company Kongō Gumi is thought to be the most ancient company in existence. There is no record of whether it had an inspiring purpose statement or an ad campaign featuring the Kendall Jenner of the early Asuka period. But the company was primarily involved in the design, construction and renovation of shrines and temples. So, even then, you might suggest there was a relationship worth discussing between business and its social purpose.

Unfortunately, after 40 generations of family ownership, Kongō Gumi went into liquidation in 2006—just missing out on the purpose age—and was purchased by the Takamatsu Construction Group. The group's website includes a 'Management credo' which goes: "We conduct the construction business as a mutually complimentary activity vital to society." It even has an official Raison d'Etre: "We shall appropriately lead the management of all Group Companies to lead into growth of our Group and to contribute to the society."

So you could say purpose has deep roots.

But bartering and trading go back further still.

One early thought leader on the ethics of commerce met his end after angrily disrupting the selling of doves, cattle and sheep in a Jerusalem temple. The Occupy Wall Street protestor of his day, he fashioned a whip from cords, drove the money changers from the temple, and "said unto them that sold doves, Take these things hence; make not my Father's house a house of merchandise." (John 2:15-16)

A week later, Jesus was on the cross. Some scholars believe the temple incident was the tipping point: preach your gospel to your cult if you like, but don't mess with the markets.

For all that, it's worth saying that Jesus wasn't necessarily a proto-anti-capitalist. By most readings, his issue was not with the idea of trading itself, but with its location and the lack of respect for discrete realms. The temple is for worship; the market is for commerce.

In an earlier incident, Jesus made a similar distinction when cornered in an impromptu Q&A with a group of Pharisees and Herodians, who were attempting to trick him into supporting insurrection. Should Jewish people pay the taxes demanded by the Roman emperor, or is that a heresy against the authority of God? Fully expecting Jesus to back a tax rebellion and invite the consequences, the questioners were bemused when Jesus first called them hypocrites and then asked to see a Roman coin. Examining the head and inscription, Jesus asked who they represented. "Caesar," replied his questioners. "Render therefore unto Caesar the things that are Caesar's, and unto God the things that are God's," said Jesus. In the modern parlance, the questioners were totally owned by this riposte and decided to leave Jesus alone.

I remember listening to both these stories in the days when I'd trudge to church every Sunday. (I'm a cultural Catholic from north-west England, no longer practising, but content to be coloured by it in various ways.) Apart from the unusual flash of anger in the temple, what stuck in my head was the logical clarity of Jesus's position, and the respect for distinct realms of human activity. There's a certain 'debate me, bro' wit about his answer to his questioners—neither a rebellion nor an endorsement, but a synthesis that allows for different authorities to be respected within, and not beyond, their own realms.

Some readers will have guessed that I'll invoke these stories later in the book, when discussing a certain purpose-driven multinational, whose products include Dove.

God and profit

Religion continues to play a role in the story of western business, which we can trace to 14th-century Tuscany and Francesco Datini, otherwise known as the Merchant of Prato. Detailed records survive of his life of trading, indicating that he was a pioneer of double-entry bookkeeping. At the top of each ledger is the motto: "In the name of God and of profit"—a sign that the purpose/profit tension was there at the start. Late in his life, struck by guilt at his accumulated wealth,

Datini gave his fortune to a social foundation, placing him in a long tradition of business people who ruthlessly accumulated wealth before engaging in philanthropy to balance the karma. Centuries later, John Rockefeller, Henry Ford, Andrew Carnegie and Bill Gates would do something similar.

By some readings of free-market capitalism, this is a perfectly rational and realist way to think about business as an indirect force for good. Concentrate on the core business, generate wealth, and, if you wish, use your position to undertake large acts of philanthropy. Even without the philanthropy, your business will generate wealth for your employees, who can support their own families and causes. And you'll pay a fair share of tax into the public coffer, while helping sustain entire communities and towns—even building them from scratch, in the case of William Lever and Port Sunlight, Titus Salt and Saltaire, or the Cadbury family and Bourneville. All this by selling products that improve people's lives in some mundane way, whether it's soap or soft drinks. What's not to like? According to the dictum of Adam Smith, 18th-century economist and philosopher of the Scottish Enlightenment, this is all an ingenious hack for human nature: "It is not from the benevolence of the butcher, the brewer, or the baker, that we expect our dinner, but from their regard to their own interest."

By this reading, the market is a clever system for distributed decision-making, from which the common good will emerge. Rather than setting prices centrally, based on predictions of supply and demand, you cascade those decisions down to billions of individuals to work out amongst themselves. The most radical free marketeer would argue this is all you need: step back and trust the market to settle on the happiest arrangement for everyone involved. To invoke Adam Smith's other dictum, we just need the "invisible hand" of the market to incentivise individuals, all of whom are acting in their own self-interest, to produce net-positive social outcomes.

Most agree it's not quite that simple. A free market is an oxymoron, in the sense that all markets need governing rules. It's the role of government and society at large to set the bounds within which the market operates, and to pay heed to the externalities that the market fails to address—the most obvious example being climate change. But as long as that balance is managed, the best role business can play is to pursue success within the rules of the game, rather than take it on itself to shape the society that should be shaping business.

Even the more left-leaning interventionist John Maynard Keynes saw the logic of the invisible hand for most of the time, but emphasised the inevitability of state intervention when markets failed. As he saw it, that intervention had to come from outside, rather than from within—and it couldn't be left to the good intentions of business leaders. In his 1930 essay Economic Possibilities for our Grandchildren, Keynes argued that there might be some distant day when businesses could prioritise 'good', but in the meantime idealistic (what we would now call 'purposeful') leaders were a menace to that progress. "Avarice and usury and precaution must be our gods for a little longer still," he warned. As Keynes saw it, the road to heaven was paved with bad intentions. Greed wasn't exactly good, but it was useful.

Proto-purpose

Not all business leaders have agreed. There is a long tradition of proto-purpose that goes back to at least the early 19th century and operates on the principle that business can be much more than an *indirect* driver of social good.

Robert Owen was one of the early reformers, introducing enlightened working practices at New Lanark Mills in Scotland, including shorter working hours, generous health plans, and the cessation of childhood labour. The world was astonished at his ability to combine making a profit with these acts of magnanimity, and for a while Owen must have thought he'd established a new model for capitalism that would catch on worldwide. But all the while, Owen was assailed by critics from both the right (this was a dangerous undermining of the market) and the left (Marx and Engels labelled him a bourgeois capitalist who kept his workers in a paternalistic prison). Owen later became dejected and increasingly unhinged, emigrating to Indiana to found a doomed utopian community, before returning to England. New Lanark Mills hit trouble and Owen's life ended in failure. But out of the ruins came the seeds of the co-operative movement, which survives to this day. The ledger of Owen's life, like that of most lives, is a complex one.

A similar story played out with William Lever, founder of Lever Bros, the company that would go on to become Unilever. Raised in the smog-filled industrial town of Bolton, Lever became the world's first soap magnate, capitalising on an era when cleanliness was increasingly prized by the Victorian middle class. An early believer in mass marketing, branded packaging and commercial jingles, he built a thriving business and invested in a new town, Port Sunlight, to house workers on the banks of the River Mersey. Lever was a passionate advocate of fresh air, to the point where he and his wife would sleep in an open-air bedroom in all weathers, a habit that is thought to have led to his wife's early death from pneumonia.

Lever's increasingly autocratic management style would eventually run into trouble, leading him to get caught up in price-fixing scandals and a doomed investment in two Outer Hebridean islands, where he tried and failed to create an industrial utopia for the 30,000 inhabitants. His overstretched company was brought low by the 1929 stock market crash and there was even a growing backlash against Port Sunlight, with one union leader commenting: "No man of an independent turn of mind can breathe for long the atmosphere of Port Sunlight... The profit-sharing scheme not only enslaves and degrades the workers, it tends to make them servile and sycophant." Like his wife before him, Lever died of pneumonia, and his company would go on to merge with Dutch company Margarine Unie.

Owen and Lever's stories, along with many others, are recounted in James O'Toole's The Enlightened Capitalists, which tells the tales of proto-purposeful entrepreneurs including John Spedan Lewis (formidable founder of John Lewis), Levi Strauss (Bavarian Jewish pioneer of the American dream), Michael Marks (Russian Jewish founder of Marks and Spencer, later canonised as St Michael) and Milton Hershey (candy bar philanthropist and mass marketing sceptic)—right up to modern-day pioneers including Anita Roddick (founder of Body Shop) and Yvon Chouinard (founder of Patagonia, to whom we'll return).

The subtitle of O'Toole's book is Cautionary Tales of Business Pioneers Who Tried to Do Well by Doing Good. And it's significant that these are cautionary tales. O'Toole writes from the perspective of a sincere believer in a better form of capitalism, but an increasingly rueful accepter that it rarely works out. Most stories meet a "sad, bad end" as O'Toole puts it, and even the best cases fail to create a model that outlasts one or two generations of charismatic leaders. Something in the nature of corporate life and market forces means the square peg of good intentions never quite makes it through the round hole of the limited company—at least not without getting severely bent out of shape.

Not-so-limited companies

'Limited company' is a phrase worth exploring, because companies haven't always been so limited. From around 1600 to 1800, chartered companies roamed the Earth: associations of investors and shareholders that were incorporated and granted exclusive rights by royal charter. Trade, exploitation and colonisation duly followed.

Prominent among them was the Dutch East India Company, established in 1602 and worth the equivalent of $8 trillion in present-day dollars at its height. Effectively the first multinational corporation, the company had the power to maintain armies, wage war, imprison and execute convicts, strike its own coins, make treaties, and establish colonies. It's interesting to wonder what a Unilever or Facebook would do with such powers today.

There were others too: the British East India Company, the South Sea Company, the Hudson's Bay Company, which survives in a different form today, and many more. All became corporate monoliths on a vast scale, with quasi-governmental powers exceeding those of small states. Chartered corporations were a testament to the untrammelled power of the profit motive when given free rein—or free enough, as long as they served their nation's interests.

The mid-nineteenth-century invention of the limited liability company came partly as a response to that awesome and awful precedent.

The gift of limited liability has been an immensely productive one, allowing entrepreneurs to take risks that yield great rewards, while being personally protected from the worst of the downsides. Open a restaurant chain, incorporate it as a limited company, and if a waiter slips and breaks his back one day, the business might be liable, but not you personally. Without that protection, it would be hard to get anything of any scale off the ground.

But from day one, the proponents of limited companies knew that this was a big concession by society. The fear was that it could lead to reckless risk-taking and a dangerous lack of accountability—and few people wanted a world of corporate leviathans taking on more power than governments. So limited liability came with heavy restrictions: make sure the objectives of your company are stated clearly and precisely, then stick to them. Declare your directors, officers and shareholders. Submit annual reports and returns. Have your accounts externally audited. This was part of the social contract: we're giving you this gift, but don't get carried away. It's strictly business—don't start any of that taking prisoners and maintaining your own armies stuff. Stay in your lane.

We've already seen how this argument plays into the purpose debate. In the politest way possible, purpose has been a way to step out of that lane, in the guise of 'stepping up' to solve society's problems. These days, companies may get entangled in culture wars more than the real thing, but the consequences go deeper than passing headlines. Companies don't take prisoners, but some employees feel trapped by a culture of political intolerance, where the company's 'values' trump their own. Companies don't execute convicts, but they have the power to fire employees for expressing political views, or debank their customers for having the wrong politics. Companies don't make treaties, but they write high-minded manifestos and join forces to sign a Statement on the Purpose of the Corporation (2019). Among the 136 signatories was Alex Gorsky, chief executive of Johnson & Johnson, who later reported that, during the process of agreeing on the statement, "There were times when I felt like Thomas Jefferson."[3]

All this plays into evolving debates about the relationship between business and society. We'll soon get into the post-2008 period and the rise of purpose itself. But first, there's an extra log of history to throw on the fire.

Stakeholders and shareholders

On 13 September 1970, the New York Times published an article by Milton Friedman, titled 'A Friedman Doctrine: The Social Responsibility of Business Is to Increase Its Profits'. In it, the conservative economist makes an argument that Adam Smith would have recognised when he wrote The Wealth of Nations in 1776. The basic case is that businesses serve society most effectively by sticking to business. At best, talk of 'social responsibility' is a shallow cover story, usually put forward by corporate executives who don't understand politics especially well. At worst, the agenda of social responsibility (what would now be called 'purpose') is a betrayal of the fiduciary duty owed by executives to shareholders, and an undemocratic exercise in forcing through a narrow political agenda. The article concludes:

> "But the doctrine of 'social responsibility' taken seriously would extend the scope of the political mechanism to every human activity. It does not differ in philosophy from the most explicitly collectivist doctrine. It differs only by professing to believe that collectivist ends can be attained without collectivist means. That is why, in my book 'Capitalism and Freedom', I have called it a 'fundamentally subversive doctrine' in a free society, and have said that in such a society, 'there is one and only one social responsibility of business—to use its resources and engage in activities designed to increase its profits so long

as it stays within the rules of the game, which is to
say, engages in open and free competition without
deception or fraud.'"

Friedman's legacy continues to be the subject of debate.
In broad brushstrokes, the story of the 20th century is one of
three economists: Friedrich Hayek, free market purist; John
Maynard Keynes, social democrat who argued for periodic
government intervention as a corrective to free market
excesses; and Milton Friedman who, alongside Hayek,
pushed back on Keynes and gave rise to the neoliberal era of
Reagan, Thatcher and beyond.

The closer you zoom in, the subtler the debate gets. Hayek
himself saw Friedman as closer to Keynes than he was to
Hayek. And in the extract above, it's notable that Friedman
talks about the 'rules of the game', which are ultimately set
by government. As we've already seen, the 'free market'
has never really existed. Markets rely on constraints that are
agreed and enforceable. If they're perfectly free, they fail.
The difference between Keynes and Friedman is never quite
as simple as a left-right divide.

But returning to the broad brushstrokes, the Friedman
article was hailed as a masterful defence of the free market,
and laid the intellectual foundations for the Reagan-Thatcher
era, with the two key quotes of the decade: "There is no such
thing as society"—Margaret Thatcher, 1987; and "Greed is
good"—Gordon Gekko, in the film Wall Street, also 1987.

Friedman's article became one pole in a binary argument
that escalated following its publication. On one side
was Friedman's 'shareholder capitalism'—the idea that

businesses were answerable to their shareholders and served society best by staying in their lane. On the other was 'stakeholder capitalism'—the idea that businesses were answerable not just to shareholders, but to everyone else: employees, customers, suppliers, communities, and the entire planet on whose resources they rely. As we'll see, the purpose debate is largely a reframing of this older argument.

On the stakeholder side were people like Klaus Schwab, author of Stakeholder Capitalism: A Global Economy that Works for Progress, People and Planet (2020). Back in 1971, as Friedman's article was being absorbed by the world, Schwab was busy setting up the European Management Forum, which would go on to become the World Economic Forum. The organisation's mission was to "improve the state of the world by engaging business, political, academic, and other leaders of society to shape global, regional, and industry agendas". Each year, the mission would be furthered by a gathering of the great and good at Davos—the annual Woodstock for stakeholder capitalists.

On its surface, stakeholder capitalism is an appealing idea. Who could disagree that businesses should consider more people than just their shareholders? Surely it's their responsibility to consider how their activities impact the people around them and the planet we all share?

But critics argue that the concept gets fuzzier the more you zoom in. In what sense are any of us truly stakeholders in, say, Unilever or Procter & Gamble? We don't have any stake in the sense of a vote or financial interest. We don't receive any salary or dividend. No one checks with us about any decisions made, and there are no rules about which stakeholders matter most when conflicts of interest inevitably arise. Instead, CEOs are able to claim the moral authority of 'stakeholders', without being answerable to any of them. And when push comes to shove, if the interests of any given stakeholders compete with the interests of shareholders, how can an executive board lean towards the former without breaking its fiduciary duty to the latter?

This argument has been bubbling for decades, far beyond Klaus Schwab. In 1972, Antoine Riboud, founder and president of Danone, made a widely reported speech to French industry leaders, in which he issued an explicit rebuke to Friedman, declaring that "corporate responsibility doesn't end at the factory gate or the company door".[4] By 2020, Danone had grown into a $40 billion business, now under the purposeful leadership of CEO Emmanuel Faber. His signature achievement was to give Danone the new legal status of 'enterprise à mission', with social purpose written into its corporate bylaws. In a triumphant speech to shareholders, Faber channelled the spirit of Antoine Riboud as he declared: "You have toppled the statue of Milton Friedman here today!"[5]

Six months later, the shareholders toppled Emmanuel Faber. By March 2021, investors were unhappy with the company's chronic underperformance, Faber was ousted as Chairman and CEO, and the Financial Times called the whole story "a case study in the pitfalls of purpose".[6]

It's one example of how most purpose stories have layers of history beneath them. The purpose debate is haunted by the ghosts of Friedman, Riboud, Keynes, Hayek, Robert Owen, William Lever, Adam Smith and many more, right back to

Francesco Datini in Tuscany and Jesus Christ in the temple.

But now we need to talk about how and when the p-word emerged.

The road to 2008

In 1976, a young trader joined New York investment bank First Boston. Having once harboured political ambitions, he entered the world of high finance and was soon leading a division specialising in the emerging field of mortgage-backed securities. Over the next decade, the young trader's rise was rapid. Some estimate he was responsible for adding $1 billion to First Boston's bottom line. Soon he became something of a Wall Street legend, pioneering what would become a multi-trillion-dollar debt-securitisation mega-market—one that involved purchasing mortgages, car and credit-card loans from banks, then slicing them up, repackaging them and selling them to thousands of other investors. It was all highly innovative. But in 1986, the legend made a high-stakes prediction about interest rates that turned out to be erroneous and cost his company at least $100 million. He was unceremoniously ousted, in a fall from grace as rapid as his rise to power. Smarting from his professional wounds, he founded a new investment management company, and called it BlackRock.

Larry Fink has already made an appearance in this book. He is the same purposeful leader who now issues letters to the corporate world, stating that "Society is demanding that companies, both public and private, serve a social purpose" and "Purpose is not a mere tagline or marketing campaign; it is a company's fundamental reason for being."

Fink had kept a lower profile throughout the 1990s and early 2000s. But then came the financial crisis of 2008, caused by the subprime mortgage crisis that came from the innovative trade of mortgage-backed securities that Fink had pioneered. Now the US government contracted BlackRock to help clean up the mess. Over the next several years, BlackRock developed close relationships with government, and Fink came close to fulfilling his political ambitions when he was lined up to become Treasury Secretary by presidential hopeful Hillary Clinton.

An unexpected electoral defeat in 2016 meant this never quite came to pass. But in the meantime, BlackRock was gaining unprecedented market power, eventually controlling up to $10 trillion in assets that flowed through multinationals around the world. None of this was BlackRock's money: they managed it on behalf of ordinary household investors. But Fink was keen to ensure that it was managed purposefully, embracing a socially progressive agenda that encouraged companies to step up to fill the void left by failed politicians. In his 2018 letter, titled 'A Sense of Purpose', Fink wrote: "We also see many governments failing to prepare for the future, on issues ranging from retirement and infrastructure to automation and worker retraining. As a result, society increasingly is turning to the private sector and asking that companies respond to broader societal challenges." By this account, the corporate takeover of societal challenges wasn't

Fink's idea. It was all due to upward pressure from the public—the same public that had just unexpectedly voted for Trump. The message now was unequivocal: "Without a sense of purpose, no company, either public or private, can achieve its full potential."

Fink appeared on the cover of Bloomberg Markets in 2017, along with a cover quote that echoed the emerging identity politics of the time, but with an interesting twist. Fink's words: "I don't identify as powerful." The next year, Fink ranked no.28 on the Forbes list of the World's Most Powerful People, ahead of Rupert Murdoch, Kim Jong-un and Vice President Mike Pence. Hillary Clinton didn't feature.

Rise of the p-word

I tell this story not because purpose is the brainchild of Larry Fink, nor to suggest he is the figurehead of an ingenious global conspiracy. But his timeline neatly captures the arc of the story, from the early age of neoliberalism through to the reckoning of 2008, then the subsequent rise of the purpose meme. When the financial crisis struck, purpose was the answer embraced by business in order to defend itself from punitive regulation—and that defensive story soon became a successful offensive move to seize the initiative and turn a weakness into a strength. Yes, corporate malfeasance caused this mess. But let's not focus on the past: look at the political crisis we're in now. Our politicians are failing us and corporations need to step up. We're not your enemy, Occupy Wall Street crowds, we're your most powerful allies.

But business didn't pluck the purpose word from nowhere. The idea had already been germinating for several years. Following the dotcom crash of 2000-2002, the corporate and marketing worlds were experiencing a crisis of confidence and yearned for something more substantive. After years of inflating the dotcom bubble with wildly hyped marketing for doomed enterprises such as boo.com, pets.com and flooz. com, the marketing industry understandably longed for clients who had something real to sell.

A few mentions of purpose began to appear. It's all about the "purpose-idea" wrote Mark Earls in Welcome to the Creative Age (2002). "The second component, the brand purpose, considers how the world could be a better place as a consequence of the brand," wrote Leslie de Chernatony in The Marketing Book (2003). "A brand with purpose is not just conducting commerce; it's driven by a mission," wrote Kevin Clark in Brandscendence (2004).

On a larger scale, increasing concerns about climate change surfaced in the Who Cares Wins report published by the United Nations in 2004. The report introduced the principles of ESG (Environment, Social and Governance) to the world, and suggested that investors would make higher profits in the long run if they placed more emphasis on environmental and social progress.

The ESG agenda would become a central pillar in the rise of purpose, enthusiastically embraced by Larry Fink and BlackRock, among many others. In 2018, BlackRock appointed Tariq Fancy to become its first Chief Investment

Officer for Sustainable Investing, heading up its ESG-based investment activity around the world. In 2019, Tariq Fancy left BlackRock and began sounding the alarm bell about an agenda that he had seen up close and found to be worse than useless. In a three-part Medium post titled The Secret Diary of a Sustainable Investor, Tariq Fancy makes a compelling case for the ESG complex acting as an active blocker of real progress, especially on questions of climate. Despite several invitations, Larry Fink has declined to engage in the debate.

But we are jumping ahead. For now, we can say that purpose was an idea blowing in the wind before the financial earthquake of 2007-2008. Soon the business world was thrown into crisis. Protestors flooded into Wall Street to demand economic justice. Occupy Wall Street united people of all backgrounds and identities. "We are the 99%!" came the cry as the movement reached its height in 2011. Soon that 99% would fragment into a network of competing identity causes: feminism, #metoo, racial justice, sex and gender, and the intersectional overlaps between them. For all that these were righteous causes, they were also easier for a corporate world to digest, compared to the economic pushback that threatened the foundations. In the language of public relations, purpose was an opportunity to reframe the narrative.

The marketing world was ready to step up.

The story of why

At the turn of the century, Simon Sinek was an adman, working at Euro RSCG (now Havas Worldwide) and Ogilvy & Mather, before launching his own consultancy in 2002. It's common practice in adland to come up with proprietary models that capture the way a brand works. On whiteboards from London to New York, you will find brand onions, brand pyramids, brand houses and brand doughnuts. Sinek's version was three concentric circles: with the 'why' of the brand at the core, circled by the 'what' and the 'how'.

In an ambitious reference to the golden ratio, he dubbed this the Golden Circle and pondered whether it might be the hidden pattern underlying all successful brands and leaders. It lay on the shelf for a while, but then Sinek describes a eureka moment when he realised this model might have echoes in neurobiology.

The initial source wasn't a neurobiologist, but California actress, Democrat activist and former wife of Dennis Hopper, Victoria Duffy Hopper—daughter of two neuroscientists. Seated next to her at an event, Sinek fell into conversation about the structure of the brain, learning how the outer, rational neocortex was wrapped around the primal, emotional limbic system. "And I realised... that the way the brain works, and the way my little model was articulated—the why, how, what—perfectly overlapped. In other words, I had discovered why marketing works. I had discovered why people do what they do. And that profoundly changed my life."[7]

Sinek sought confirmation from a neuroscientist,

appropriately named Peter Whybrow. It turned out the model wasn't quite a perfect overlap: Whybrow advised Sinek to flip the order of the how and the what. But apart from that, there was just enough science to give Sinek confidence in his model, or his 'discovery' as he preferred to call it. "It's not my opinion, it's biology," he later wrote.

The biology is contested. Sinek's version comes from the 'triune' model of the brain, popularised by neuroscientist Paul MacLean in the 1960s. The idea is that our 'lizard brain' is the most primitive, non-verbal part that functions on instinct. Over the course of evolution, this was enveloped by the ancient limbic system, source of our emotions. More recently, this was encased in a sophisticated neocortex that separates our brains from those of other vertebrates and allows us to make rational, verbal decisions. If you want to inspire people to buy into your brand, you need to dig past the what and the how and get to the why, where the real action happens. "People don't buy what you do, they buy why you do it," Sinek repeats eight times in his book, Start With Why.

Sinek's advisor, Peter Whybrow, subscribes to MacLean's triune model. In 1997, Whybrow published A Mood Apart, including a chapter on the lizard brain that opens with a quote from MacLean. And in 2010, Whybrow published another paper, titled 'After Freud: What do neuroscience advances tell us about human nature?', which shows continued faith in MacLean's ideas. Sample quote:

> "The human brain is not a single organ but a hybrid:
> an evolved hierarchy of three-brains-in-one. Thus

human behavior is best understood when brain anatomy is placed within an evolutionary context. A primitive 'lizard' brain, designed millennia ago for survival, lies at the core of the human brain and cradles the roots of ancient dopamine reward pathways that are the superhighways of pleasure, curiosity and desire."

Even when Sinek published Start With Why in 2009, this triune model had long fallen out of favour. A 2008 article in the Yale School of Medicine journal is titled 'A theory abandoned but still compelling'. The article discusses how the science has been debunked, but "the force of MacLean's personality gave his ideas a special resonance".

More recently, celebrated neuroscientist Lisa Feldman Barrett included a dismantling of the triune brain myth in her book Seven and a Half Lessons About the Brain (2020), which you can hear her discussing with fellow neuroscientist Sam Harris on episode 247 of his Making Sense podcast. As she writes elsewhere: "This model, called the triune brain, is a fantasy... The brain didn't evolve in layers like sedimentary rocks. Rather (in the words of the neuroscientist Georg Striedter), brains evolve like companies do: they reorganise as they expand. The brain regions that MacLean considered emotional, which he referred to as the 'limbic system', are now known to contain major hubs for general communication throughout the brain. They control the various systems of the body, and they're important for many phenomena besides emotion, such as including language, concepts, stress, and even the coordination of the five senses into a cohesive experience."[8]

I include this scientific detour because I've yet to see a debunking of Sinek's 'discovery' anywhere else. This may be a case of Brandolini's Law, which states that 'The amount of energy needed to refute bullshit is an order of magnitude bigger than that needed to produce it'. There are deep questions about the relationship between emotion, thought and language, but those questions are not reducible to a cartoon model that claims to reveal the truth of humans, marketing, business or anything else.

Nevertheless, Sinek's book made a deep impression on the business and marketing worlds, aided by a TED talk that became one of the most viewed of all time. From the start, Sinek's idea of 'why' was synonymous with purpose—"By why, I mean 'What's your purpose, cause, belief'". Its power was that it flattered business leaders into seeing themselves as heroes driven by a higher cause, of which business was just the outward expression. And the beauty of the theory was that anyone puzzled by the 'why' question was simply confirming Sinek's model: it's meant to be hard to answer, because it lies deep in the non-verbal brain.

So if you ask the boss of a widget company, "Why do you do what you do?" she might be nonplussed by the obviousness of the answer: "Well, we do it to sell widgets and make a living, and there was a gap in the market for widgets." Or she might be forced to grope around for some faux-psychological origin story: "I guess I saw a gap in the market for widgets, and became passionate about how… people had been living for so long without widgets of this particular kind… at this particular price point… so I wanted to... democratise?.. the widgets and maybe... break the taboo?.. around the widgets, and... make people's lives easier with the widgets... and I definitely want to sell the widgets to everyone... so I guess I'm on a mission to improve life for everyone, everywhere... and encourage the world to... widget itself happy™?" Soon the widget company has recast itself as a 'challenge the status quo' company that just happens to make widgets.

This sounds like a parody, but it's the story that Sinek projects back onto Apple (his favoured example of a start-with-why company). The other two leading case studies in his business book don't come from the business world.

First, there are the Wright brothers. Sinek's version of events is that they won the race to develop the first motor-powered airplane because they were driven by a stronger internal sense of 'why':

> "It wasn't luck. Both the Wright brothers and [their rival] Langley were highly motivated. Both had a strong work ethic. Both had keen scientific minds. They were pursuing exactly the same goal, but only the Wright brothers were able to inspire those around them and truly lead their team to develop a technology that would change the world. Only the Wright brothers started with Why."

So a fascinating story of incremental engineering innovation is flattened into a simple question of desire—Sinek writes like a sports commentator who declares that the winning team 'wanted it more'. Meanwhile, he overlooks a key aspect of the Wright brothers' story, which ought to interest the business community he's addressing. There's a reason we're not all flying on Wright Airlines. Larry Tise, historian and Wright brothers biographer, sums it up like this:

> "Most historians treat the Wright Brothers as great American heroes. I see them partly as tragic figures. Once they had the invention, they wanted to be like Henry Ford and Alexander Graham Bell and become rich off their invention and work. They got the patent on their flying machine, and then they didn't work to further flight. They worked to protect the patent. They became obsessed with making money and protecting the patent."[9]

There is nothing wrong with this desire to monetise their work, but you have to squint hard to see a 'start with why' narrative anywhere in the picture.

The other example is Martin Luther King—which, no doubt unfairly, brings to mind David Brent's admiration of Nelson Mandela in British comedy The Office. On the face of it, this one stands up better. As Sinek notes, King said "I have a dream", not "I have a plan". But if that dream was King's 'why', it was one he shared with many who went before him. Sinek's view misreads the true dynamic of King's Lincoln Memorial address, where the line immediately following the first instance of "I have a dream" is: "It is a dream deeply rooted in the American dream."

Throughout the speech, King anchors his case not in his

own inner 'why', but in the values of the audience he is trying to persuade. Emancipation wasn't a threat to the American dream, he argued, but instead represented its true fulfilment:

> "When the architects of our republic wrote the magnificent words of the Constitution and the Declaration of Independence, they were signing a promissory note to which every American was to fall heir. This note was a promise that all men — yes, Black men as well as white men — would be guaranteed the unalienable rights of life, liberty and the pursuit of happiness."

This is the clear 'what' and 'how' that runs throughout the speech. You have the what: the Constitution, the Declaration of Independence, the Emancipation Proclamation, the Christian values, the liberal tradition. This is 'how' you live up to them.

All this is a contested area, and King's speech was only one moment in a lifetime of tough political activism. But reducing his life to an inspirational parable for CEOs is unserious.

A year after the publication of his book, Sinek recorded an interview with Adam Fish on anthropology podcast Savage Minds.[10] He recounts the origin story of the Golden Circle, then moves on to wider thoughts about the distinction between for-profit and not-for-profit organisations, and the nature of corporate leadership.

Some might wonder if the existence of not-for-profits is a problem for Sinek's idea of purpose-driven companies. After all, if you were truly driven by a higher purpose that goes beyond profit, wouldn't you choose to be a not-for-profit in the first place? But for Sinek, it's a matter of language:

> "All organisations are for-profit; it's just how they measure their profit that's different. For-profits measure their profit in dollars and cents; not-for-profits measure their profit in terms of making a particular impact in the world."

This curious distinction leads Sinek into further thoughts about the superiority of for-profits when it comes to executing on their cause:

> "You talk to non-profits all the time and they're carrying a lot of dead weight in terms of talent, but they are loath to fire anybody because they're so devoted to the cause. But in reality they're bad employees. A for-profit would have no problem trimming out dead wood because they need people who produce. It's the social entrepreneur who understands that what you need to do is combine those models. Strong on cause and strong on structure. Not one or the other: two sides of the same coin… The best organisations function as if they were social movements."

Many will recognise the criticisms of the not-for-profit world, which can be prone to institutional inertia. For Sinek, the answer is not to improve that world, but to look instead to cause-driven corporations. And the way they should function is through strong, purposeful leadership, not consensus or democracy.

> "Consensus-driven organisations don't work... The best form of government is the benevolent dictatorship. And the same is true in organisations. The whole idea of consensus is lowest common denominator. How do you please as many people as possible? You end up with something incredibly diluted. Look at any congressional bill that passes... Rare are the bills that are truly profound and great because you have to please as many people and as many constituents as possible. So a leader is the single person, or no more than a pair of people, at the top, who explains their vision of the world and asks those in their organisation who believe what they believe to help build it. Consensus is not the way. There is only one vision and there can be only one vision."

There is only one vision and there can be only one vision. This is where Sinek's model of social purpose ends up: for-profits grappling with social causes based on the gut feelings of their benevolently dictatorial leaders, with the idea of employee consensus a tiresome distraction. It might be an efficient way to make decisions on the price of your widgets or the location of your warehouse. But when it comes to adopting social causes, and pushing a 'make the world a better place' agenda, many would see the benefits of slow political consensus, based on the same Constitution that Martin Luther King embraced.

Sinek has much to teach the marketing world, but none of it is about purpose. His skill lies in marketing and rhetoric. He knows the power of a three-word imperative slogan (Just Do It... Take Back Control... Start With Why); he knows the power of repetition (note the many examples in the TED talk); he knows the importance of scienceyness to persuasion (like the 1920s marketer who unearthed the obscure term 'halitosis' to start selling Listerine); he knows words like 'discovery' are more powerful than 'theory'; he knows that branding himself an 'optimist' is a power move to cast any questioners as pessimists and cynics; he has the gift of spoken fluency that makes his ideas more compelling in person than on the page.

And he knows that people generally don't look at evidence claims too closely. There is one final piece we need to look at before completing this history.

Hard, clean numbers

In October 2008, a month after the collapse of Lehman Brothers, and around the time that the UK government was pulling Royal Bank of Scotland back from the brink, Jim Stengel announced he was stepping down as Chief Marketing Officer at Procter & Gamble. According to his author biography, "This bold move was Jim's first step on a new mission to share his passion for growing business through a focus on higher ideals."

The result was Grow: How Ideals Power Growth and Profit at the World's 50 Greatest Companies (Crown Business, 2011). It became one of the foundational texts of the purpose movement, cited by Simon Sinek and endorsed by back cover quotes from Sheryl Sandberg, then COO at Facebook ("A new, powerful model for business") and Martin Sorrell, then CEO at advertising giant WPP, who described himself as "utterly convinced". He continued: "Jim Stengel shares his beliefs and his experience with a generosity bordering on the reckless; and has the hard, clean numbers to bear his teachings out."

These hard, clean numbers came from research conducted by Millward Brown, then part of Kantar, WPP's 'insight, information and consultancy' group. Jim Stengel asked them to look into whether a strong sense of ideals was related to better business performance.

Although he uses the word 'ideal', it's clear Stengel is operating on a similar definition to 'purpose', complete with its social dimension: "We define ideal as the higher-order benefit a brand or a business gives to the world," says Stengel. "At the heart of every business, every brand, is a reason we exist. A higher ideal. A mission in the world… It's not a marketing slogan, it's not an ad campaign. It's why you are here." Later, Stengel uses the two terms synonymously, talking of how "businesses driven by a higher ideal, a higher purpose, outperform their competition by a wide margin".

At this point, it's worth pausing and asking yourself how you might design a study to prove Stengel's theory. Maybe you would start with a rigorous definition of 'ideal' that you could then use to identify a group of companies that are guided by one, and another group of companies that aren't. Having identified each group, you might then measure their past performance to look for meaningful differences, while being alert for other variables that could skew the results. Better still, you would want your theory to hold some predictive value, so you might monitor the future performance of your sample groups and look for sustained differences.

Stengel and Millward Brown took a different approach. First, they identified the 50 brands that "ranked highest on both consumer bonding and value creation over the past decade"—a judgment based on the top performers in Millward Brown's 50,000-strong brand database. Then they went looking for anything that might be described as an 'ideal' to explain the success of those companies.

The results were dramatic. "The study… establishes a cause and effect relationship between a brand's ability to serve a higher purpose and its financial performance. Notably, investment in these companies—the Stengel 50—over the past decade would have been 400% more profitable than an investment in the S&P 500," reported Millward Brown. The purpose case had been proven: "'Doing well by doing good'— is that really attainable? We have always thought so, but now we have proof. The most successful brands and businesses in the world are built around something other than just making profit. They are built around ideals."

We encountered Brandolini's Law in the previous section—'The amount of energy needed to refute bullshit is an order of magnitude bigger than that needed to produce it.' Professor Byron Sharp of the Ehrenberg-Bass Institute for Marketing Science did his best to summon the required energy in a 2011 post:

> "Promotional material for Stengel's book says that 'over the 2000s an investment in these companies—The Stengel 50—would have been 400% more profitable than an investment in the S&P 500'. The implication is that this proves Stengel's 'ideals' thesis—but Stengel picked these companies for their financial growth! If they had been picked purely based on some, ideally 'hard' (or intersubjectively certifiable), measure of being 'ideals driven' then correlations with financial performance might mean something. Especially if this were future, not past, performance. But as these companies were picked for their financial performance, then their stock price performance over the same period shows nothing."[11]

Years later, with the Stengel 50 still widely hailed as proof of the growing purpose movement, behavioural scientist and author Richard Shotton offered another deconstruction, citing five issues.[12]

First, the brand isn't the business. As Shotton patiently explains, several brands in Stengel's list don't even have an individual share price, but are part of larger companies. One of them is Stonyfield Farm, which accounted for less than 2% of Danone's revenue in 2014. Stengel's strange theory is that Danone's share price rose because of Stonyfield Farm's brand ideal. Similar problems apply to at least 12 of the 50.

Second, the logic is circular. As Shotton slightly less patiently explains, the Stengel 50 comes from picking the best 0.1% from Millward Brown's 50,000-strong database: "It's not surprising that those brands performed well in terms of share price. If they hadn't performed well in the past they wouldn't be in Millward Brown's top 0.1% of brands. Stengel's finding, if you re-state it at its most basic, is that brands that feature in the top 0.1% of companies have performed well in the stock market. That's circular logic."

Third, the definition is retro-fitted. Stengel's definition of 'ideal' is loose to the point of parody. Moët & Chandon 'exists to transform occasions into celebrations'. Mercedes-Benz 'exists to epitomise a life of achievement'. BlackBerry 'exists to connect people with one another and the content that is most important in their lives, anytime, anywhere'. These are the kind of anodyne category descriptors used by many brands, mostly unconnected to any kind of ground truth. Yet the study has been used countless times since to assert the importance of a social purpose to brand performance.

Fourth, there is no comparison group. At no point does Stengel compare successful brands to unsuccessful ones. How do we know whether the bottom 0.1% also had a similarly expressed ideal? How do we know whether the top performers might have had other things in common that had greater explanatory power? No one looked.

Fifth, it has no predictive value. Shotton looked at the stock market performance of the Stengel 50 over the five years following its publication. Of the 26 companies who weren't part of a larger holding company and could therefore be meaningfully measured, only 9 outperformed the S&P benchmark. By chance alone, you might expect 13.

Branding continues to operate on the vague assumption that there must be something to Stengel's book—surely there's no smoke without a fire. Brandolini suggests otherwise.

The purpose decade

Sinek and Stengel were by no means the only prophets of purpose. In the years after 2008, their books were part of a wave of purpose titles that continues to this day. A far from exhaustive list includes Philanthrocapitalism: How the Rich Can Save the World (Matthew Bishop and Michael Green, 2008), The Story of Purpose (Joey Reiman, 2012), Conscious Capitalism (John Mackey and Raj Sisodia, 2013), Do / Purpose (Dave Hieatt, 2014), Leading from Purpose (Nick Craig, 2018), Activate Brand Purpose: How to Harness the Power of Movements to Transform Your Company (Scott Goodson and Chip Walker, 2021), Purpose and Profit: How Business Can Lift Up the World (George Serafeim, 2022) and The Activist Leader (Lucy Parker and Jon Miller, 2023).

By 2017, purpose was already beginning to feel like a trend burning itself out. I made my first intervention in June 2017, with an article in Creative Review, optimistically titled 'Is this the end for brand purpose?' Around the same time, Ipsos and Trinity Mirror released consumer research highlighting a growing distrust of purposeful advertising. "A big part of the problem," reported Trinity Mirror, "is the 'arrogance' of brands adopting an ill-fitting purpose, leading to increased cynicism among consumers."[13] Meanwhile, the wave of social purpose advertising was already sufficiently familiar for Saturday Night Live to satirise it (Pitch Meeting, 2017).

In retrospect, this was the calm before the storm. Larry Fink's purposeful letters began in 2018, the US Business Roundtable signed its Statement on the Purpose of a Corporation in 2019, and purpose continued growing into the corporate leviathan that it is today. This was accompanied by growing dissent from both the left and right, including The Rise of Woke Capital (Ross Douthat, New York Times, 2018), Winners Take All (Anand Giridharadas, 2018), Can't Sell, Won't Sell (Steve Harrison, 2020), Woke, Inc (Vivek Ramaswamy, 2021), and Woke Capitalism (Carl Rhodes, 2021).

Since 2022, there has been a sense of things shifting—quiet repositionings away from purpose by the likes of Unilever and P&G, and no mention of the word in Larry Fink's 2023 annual letter. But this may be because the work is done: purpose is deeply woven into the institutional fabric of business and marketing. Visit any brand or holding company website and you are likely to find a purpose statement straining to connect what they do to wider society. Many advertising agencies and consultancies explicitly pitch themselves around purpose. Social purpose has taken over creative advertising awards schemes and established firm roots in the educational sector. The Vice Chancellor of University of the Arts London (home of the Chief Social Purpose Officer mentioned in my introduction) cited Simon

Sinek as an inspiration. At the time of writing, a glance at recent headlines includes: 'For Gen Z-ers, brand purpose means helping us impact the world' (AdAge); 'Richard Edelman: This not the end of brand purpose' (PRWeek); 'Mars CEO: Attacks on brand purpose are 'nonsense'' (Raconteur); and 'What makes a great corporate purpose statement' (Harvard Business Review).

In the name of God and of profit, said the motto on Francesco Datini's ledger.

Now purpose represents the one true path. And it's leading nowhere good.

3.
How purpose leads to
bad marketing

Thus, when you give to the needy, sound no
trumpet before you, as the hypocrites do...
that they may be praised by others.

– Matthew 6:2

A CELLIST PLAYS ON a rooftop. Far below, a protest march is gathering. People of diverse ethnicities in the 18-34 age bracket walk along with beaming smiles. One holds a sign saying 'Join the conversation'. Another holds a sign in French. It says 'Faites de la conversation'. The cellist plays more passionately, sweat beads spraying from his tousle of jet black hair.

Elsewhere, a Muslim photographer is marking up her contact sheets, but looks dissatisfied. We cut to a white, blonde, former reality TV star who is involved in a glamorous photo shoot. As she poses in a doorway, she catches sight of the passing protest and a sign reading 'Love'. She grows concerned and breaks her pose.

The cellist has moved into a loft apartment with exposed brick walls. He glances out the window, takes a swig of his soft drink, and walks to the balcony to see the protest march passing below.

The Muslim photographer is frustrated. She screws up a photo and sweeps her work from the desk. Hearing the protest march passing outside, she grabs her camera and rushes onto the street. Among the protestors is a man with a cello case on his back. Some of the protestors are now breakdancing. A band forms, featuring the cellist.

Now the march continues and the glamour model catches the eye of the cellist, who nods and beckons her. The model tears off her blonde wig, smudges her lipstick and joins the marchers, who are now approaching a police line.

Weaving her way through the crowd, the model grabs a chilled can from an ice bucket, nods again at the cellist, and makes her way to the police line. The Muslim photographer is there to capture the moment as Kendall Jenner approaches the hottest police officer and hands him a cold can.

The crowd cheers ecstatically as the officer takes a swig and turns to his colleagues with a shrug and a cute smile.

The Pepsi logo appears with the endline: Live bolder. Live louder. Live for now.

***

Pepsi's commercial was released on 4 April 2017. After a social media storm of epic proportions, it was withdrawn on 5 April 2017. Pepsi was accused of co-opting and trivialising the Black Lives Matter movement that had formed in the wake of the killing of Michael Brown. Bernice King, daughter of Martin Luther King, posted an image of her father confronting an aggressive police line. "If only Daddy would have known about the power of #Pepsi" she wrote.

I remember watching the ad for the first time. My hope was that the cellist would join the march in the style of Woody Allen, in that scene where he plays a cellist in a marching band, desperately playing a few notes before grabbing his stool and shuffling forward a few steps.

It was part of what prompted me to write my first article about purpose.[14] Other examples included McDonald's telling a story of a boy bonding with his dead father over a shared love of filet o' fish, Heineken getting culture war opponents together over a product shot, Dove introducing a range of curly-haired emojis and packaging that mimicked different body shapes, and Cannes Lions celebrating the 'I Sea' app that claimed to help rescue refugees lost at sea but turned out to be a paper-thin 'proof of concept'.

By 2017, this trend for emotional, vaguely socially conscious advertising was already a painful cliché, sent up in a Saturday Night Live sketch in which two agencies pitch for the Cheetos Super Bowl campaign. The first team, played by Alec Baldwin and Aidy Bryant, pitches their killer idea: "We open on a little immigrant girl. She's dusty, she's tired, she's come a long way. She looks up and sees… a wall. How will she get over it? A boy appears at the top. He throws down a rope. The rope is made from American flags. The girl climbs the rope. She sees her new country for the first time, and she cries. Hard cut. Cheetos." The other team pitches fun ideas based on the idea of Cheetos being tasty, to the bewilderment of the client team. The gag continues as the audience laughs in recognition of a trend that has already become a laughing stock.

Purpose was entirely responsible for it. It came from brands clumsily groping around for a higher social purpose and predictably ending up way out of their comfort zone.

But this isn't primarily what I'm writing about in this chapter. It's too easy to shoot down the many examples of superficial 'purpose' advertising that featured so prominently in the 2010s. Instead, I want to focus more on the 'proper' stuff that many purpose advocates would regard as purpose done right.

Back in 2017, you might have thought the Pepsi backlash would mean the end of the purpose trend. But the response from adland was to double down. Marketers talked about how purpose advertising only works if you really mean it. Most brands subsequently decided they really, really meant it, because that's how the psychology works: we all want to feel like we're the good guys. Purpose sank deeper into every area of marketing, affecting the way brands thought about themselves and their audiences.

Does it always lead to bad marketing? Maybe not—it would be foolish to make any categorical claim in fields as complex and over-determined as advertising and branding. It's also not my main concern in this book. In many ways, I would be *more* concerned if purpose worked in terms of delivering commercial results, because it's the social effects that are most troubling.

Nevertheless, my claim is that there are structural factors baked into the idea of purpose that significantly increase the *likelihood* of bad marketing. I will break them down in these next sections. If you're a general reader who has ever wondered why advertising is more earnest of late, this chapter may shed some light. If you're a purposeful player in the marketing world, it might be a prompt to stop striking a pose, smudge off the political lip gloss, and rejoin the real world.

Purpose leads to sameness, not difference

There is an ongoing argument in the marketing world about whether brands should aim for difference or distinctiveness.

For a long while, difference reigned supreme. The idea was to find a 'unique selling point' that identified something different about your brand, then lean into it. One wrinkle was that it might not necessarily be something unique about your product, but it needed to be unique in the sense that you were the only one saying it. In the era of tobacco advertising, Lucky Strike claimed 'It's toasted' and built a successful brand on it. Other brands were toasted too, but Lucky Strike planted its flag and claimed that mental space.

More recently, thanks to rigorous work by the Ehrenberg-Bass Institute, marketers have come to appreciate that distinctiveness is at least equally, and probably far more, important. You don't need to build from a product claim that is meaningfully different. You can just be distinctive in the sense of always being the orange brand, or always using the same typeface, or repeating a sonic jingle at the end of your ads. Think of these as your 'distinctive assets' and use them: they build memory structures in the minds of customers, so that they vaguely remember your brand and have positive associations next time they're idly picking something from the shelf. The shelf is physical availability. The recognition is mental availability. Get them both right and you have a fighting chance.

Outsiders may be surprised to know this difference vs distinctiveness argument is a fiery one in the marketing world, with people arguing over the exact difference or distinction between difference and distinctiveness.

But one thing on which everyone is agreed is that it helps to be one or the other.

Being samey, predictable, generic and unremarkable is likely to mean you're less noticed and less remembered. As with most things in marketing, there are subtleties to this—it can help to mimic the accepted codes of your sector, maybe using green to signal an eco product. But at some point you will need to find something distinctive or different that you can lodge into people's brains.

Brand purpose has a structural flaw: it tilts brands towards sameness.

Broadly, it relies on the Simon Sinek maxim that we discussed earlier: Start With Why.

When brands go in search of their 'why', or their higher reason for being, it inexorably leads up a ladder of abstraction. Or to use another analogy, it's like the homeopathy of the marketing world. It involves taking the functional purpose of any given product, diluting it to a slightly more abstract level, then diluting it again and repeating the process until you reach a level of abstraction so remote that any sense of specificity has been lost entirely.

So if your product is a bar of chocolate, it's not about giving people something chocolatey to eat, it's about giving them a tasty treat. And it's not about giving them a tasty treat, it's about giving them a treat in a wider sense. And it's not about the treat as such, but the enjoyment you get from that treat. And it's not about the physical enjoyment, but the emotional enjoyment. And it's not about the emotional enjoyment, but the shared emotional enjoyment. And it's not about the shared enjoyment, it's about making the world a better place through the power of sharing. And now your brand purpose is more closely aligned to Buddhism than it is to chocolate.

Meanwhile, someone else's product is a bar of soap. But it's not about getting people clean, it's about giving them a sense of cleanliness. And it's not about giving them a sense of cleanliness, it's about giving them a sense of looking good. And it's not about looking good, but feeling good. And it's not about feeling good physically, but feeling good emotionally. And it's not about feeling good emotionally, it's about making the world a better place through the power of helping everyone feel good emotionally. And now your brand purpose is pretty similar to the bar of chocolate.

You will see this pattern of thought in action when you look at the purposes of some of the biggest brands of the last decade:

We imagine a world where you can belong anywhere. We elevate the world's consciousness. We ignite opportunity by setting the world in motion. We give people the power to build community and bring the world closer together. We inspire and nurture the human spirit: one person, one cup and one neighborhood at a time. We unlock the potential of human creativity.

These are the purpose statements of six brands you know well—you might like to guess them. They include a property rental company, an office rental company, a transport company, a social media network, a coffee chain, and a music business.[15] But based on these statements, you would have little idea that they do radically different things to each other. The language is a warm soup of abstraction— consciousness, opportunity, spirit, potential, creativity— with just one crouton: the mention of a 'cup' that is a clue to the coffee chain.

Purpose statements are largely internal, but you will notice how this pattern of thought has surfaced in the slogans that brands put out into the world. Decades ago, popular slogans included 'Beanz Meanz Heinz', 'Have a break, Have a KitKat', 'Avis: We try harder', 'Ronseal: Does exactly what it says on the tin', or 'KFC: Finger lickin' good'.

Each represented a linguistic meme that brands inserted into the culture. Next time you're buying some beans, you might be more likely to equate them with Heinz, thanks to that jagged little mnemonic. Next time you're having a mid-morning coffee break, you might associate that moment (what marketers call a 'category entry point') with KitKat. Next time you're a politician trying to come across as relatable and straight-talking, you might refer to 'doing exactly what it says on the tin'.

Over the course of the 2010s, brand slogans climbed the ladder of abstraction and ended up somewhere beyond the reach of conventional language. 'Burger King: Be Your Way.' 'Stella Artois: Be Legacy.' 'Lenovo: The Do Inside.' 'Rightmove: Find Your Happy.'

Each slogan comes from the impulse to look deeply into the business and ask what it's *really* about. Dig through the neocortical 'what' and the limbic 'how' and get into the lizard brain. It's not burgers, it's self-realisation. It's not lager, it's legacy. It's not technology, it's agency. It's not moving house, it's finding happiness.

Meanwhile, somewhere far below, a customer glances up at a billboard and looks down again, with barely an impression left on their hippocampus.

Purpose misunderstands how marketing works

"Half my advertising spend is wasted. The trouble is, I don't know which half," goes the quote usually attributed to 19th-century retail magnate John Wanamaker.

Incidentally, Wanamaker was an interesting character—a conflicted philanthropist and inventor of the price tag, at a time when most buying was done through haggling. "A devout Christian, he believed that if everyone was equal before God, then everyone should be equal before price," explains his PBS biography. He appears to have believed that almost everything had a price tag. During World War One, he earnestly pushed the idea that the US should buy Belgium from Germany for $100 billion as a way to end the carnage.[16]

But back to the quote. Over a century later, marketing remains a mystery. Think of a brand like Coca-Cola or Pepsi and you will bring to mind a lifetime of associations that have accumulated over the years. Some arise because of the ads you saw; others arise *despite* the ads you saw. Maybe you're of an age where you remember a bare-chested construction worker taking a swig from a can of Diet Coke. Or maybe you associate Diet Coke with Donald Trump, because you read about him liking it. Maybe Pepsi brings back random memories of a school friend who shared a can on the bus. Or maybe you associate it with the colour blue and subliminally don't think of blue as a tasty colour. Either way, both of these brands are so ubiquitous that you might reasonably think—'OK, we get it. You can stop funnelling billions into branding, advertising and sponsorship. If I'm going to be Team Pepsi or Team Coke, believe me, I made that decision a long time ago.'

The truth of how brands work is more subtle. I've already mentioned Byron Sharp and the Ehrenberg-Bass Institute, who have done valuable work on marketing in recent years, primarily through the book How Brands Grow. We may still not understand marketing, but Byron Sharp has shown it's possible to bring some empiricism to the process. And the results are surprising, even to seasoned marketers.

Who actually makes Coca-Cola successful? You could answer this question by looking at their 'average buyer' who purchases about 12 times a year. But the average buyer is not the same as the *typical* buyer, because a few heavy buyers skew the data: around 4% of Coca-Cola's total buyers deliver 25% of total sales. When it comes to the typical buyer, it turns out half of all Coke buyers buy only one or two cans a year. And around 30% of Coke buyers don't even buy it once a year. That figure is more than 50% for Pepsi buyers.

That's quite a revelation for marketers. It's disconcerting to think that half their business relies on customers who barely ever think about them. Marketers like to talk about 'targeting' their customers or sustaining conversations with 'tribes' of people who love their brand—which might work for the 4% who were going to buy your brand anyway. But it turns out light buyers—people who barely connect with your brand all year—are crucial to your commercial success. And once you look at the whole spread, a 'heavy buyer' is anyone who buys three or more cans a year, which might not strike you as that heavy.

This radically changes the conversation that a Pepsi or a Coke is holding with the world. Rather than a dialogue between equally invested parties, it's more a continual, long-distance, low-level prod of 'We exist', 'We're the red one', 'Next time you're buying a soft drink, remember you like us', and 'Hopefully see you next year'.

As with Pepsi and Coke, so with most other brands. And the disconcerting thing for marketers is that the user base of these 'competitor' brands is pretty much the same. It's not that the world is split into Pepsi and Coke buyers. It's more that there are soft drinks buyers and most of them buy infrequently, and sometimes they grab a Pepsi, and sometimes they grab a Coke.

Into this world steps purpose. Customers are longing for a 'why', says the brand. Customers want to buy a soft drink that reflects their values, says the brand. Customers are demanding that soft drinks step up and fill the political void, says the brand. The truth is more like that Mad Men meme with Don Draper in the elevator: "I don't think about you at all."[17]

Purpose misunderstands people—especially young people

Ah, but things are changing. Gen Z is different. Gen Z is more politically engaged than ever. Gen Z demands authentic social purpose from the brands it supports.

This is an argument beloved of a certain kind of consultancy that likes to invent generational cohorts, make sweeping generalisations about how different they are, then charge vast amounts to act as the Gen Z whisperer to anxious, middle-aged clients. In 2022, public relations giant Edelman set up a Gen Z division to tap into this lucrative market. The CEO, or ZEO as they call it, is gender fluid fashion designer, Harris Reed. The COO (Chief Operating Officer) is a more conventional choice: Amanda Edelman, daughter of the Edelman CEO. Gen Z demands authenticity from its brands, including authentic nepotism.

For corporations drawn to the idea of purpose, it's a useful fiction to say this is coming from bottom-up pressure, not top-down power. Many even believe it, because they have Gen Z consultancies whispering persuasively in their ears.

Gen Z is "True Gen" says McKinsey. They see "consumption as access rather than possession, consumption as an expression of individual identity, and consumption as a matter of ethical concern".[18] "To win the hearts of Gen Z, companies and employers will need to highlight their efforts to be good global citizens," says Deloitte. "And actions speak louder than words: Companies must demonstrate their commitment to a broader set of societal challenges such as sustainability, climate change, and hunger." The good news for corporations is that this could also save on salary costs: "Gen Z values salary less than every other generation: If given the choice of accepting a better-paying but boring job versus work that was more interesting but didn't pay as well, Gen Z was fairly evenly split over the choice."[19]

It's true that many surveys suggest consumers, and Gen

Z in particular, say they want brands to align with their ethical values. 82% of shoppers "want consumer goods brand values to be aligned with their own," according to Harris Poll research commissioned by Google Cloud in 2022.[20] Similarly, PriceWaterhouseCoopers research from 2021 suggests that 84%, 76% and 80% of consumers are "more likely to buy from" companies that stand up for environmental, social and governance issues respectively.[21]

The trouble is that consumers (me included) have little insight into what makes them buy stuff. When you're asked to think about it in a survey, you would need a heart of stone to say ethical issues don't matter to you at all. At the very least, it's an awkward answer to give to the researcher on the other end of the line. But even in anonymous polling, we generally like to think well of ourselves. I'm a decent person, I do my best, yes of course ethics matter.

But glance around your home and take an inventory of all the stuff you've accumulated along the way. Consider which brand lies behind the curtains, the carpet, the microwave, the television, the shirt, the biscuits, the home insurer, the broadband provider, the salt and pepper, the deodorant, the shoes, the jars in the back of the fridge, the printer of this book, the place where you bought it (thank you). Maybe there's a Patagonia fleece between the Primark stuff in the wardrobe; maybe you went for the eco washing powder that was on offer. But by and large, we buy what we buy, and say in surveys what we say in surveys.

2022 US research into Gen Z's favourite brands suggests they're human beings like everyone else. Attitudinal surveys aside, the brands they think of most favourably are YouTube,

Google, Netflix, Amazon, M&Ms, Walmart, Target, Doritos, Kit Kat and Oreo.[22] "Actions speak louder than words," says the Deloitte report quoted above. It's certainly true when it comes to consumers.

There's another way to judge consumer sentiment when it comes to social and political issues. One of the curious features of the purpose movement in the UK and US is that it intensified shortly after consumers voted to take Britain out of Europe and put Trump into office, then continued as consumers voted first for Theresa May, then overwhelmingly for Boris Johnson, and persisted as 74 million Americans voted for Trump, the highest ever number for a losing candidate.

For these purposes, it's not necessary to take a stance on how great or depressing those results were—only to observe that the public has been broadly split down the middle when it comes to voting on big questions. But the narrative from corporations suggests universal upward pressure to embrace progressive causes. "Stakeholders are pushing companies to wade into sensitive social and political issues—especially as they see governments failing to do so effectively," says Larry Fink in his 2019 letter to CEOs. "The world needs your leadership," he continues. CEOs have duly stepped up to fill the 'political void', somehow not noticing that the void is packed with 155 million Americans who vigorously contested the 2020 election, a higher number than any in history.

Once again, the claim is that younger people are different. "What I'm here to explain… is that Gen Z as a consumer will abandon you if you're not ethical," says Clay Lute, one of the Gen Z whisperers at Z Suite, part of the Berns Communications Group.[23] He quotes a 2021 survey by market research group Forrester, which found that 51% of Gen Z consumers in the US will do research into companies to ensure they "align with their position on corporate social responsibility" before making a purchase.[24]

Again, the truth is more interesting. Three weeks after the Russian invasion of Ukraine, a UK poll by Opinium found that 81% of over-55s thought brands should stop doing business in Russia, but only 33% of 18-34 year olds.[25] Similarly, only 15% of all adults wanted brands to reflect the crisis in their advertising campaigns, and that number fell to 11% among 18-34 year olds. Yes, these questions are also asking consumers to examine their own motives, which doesn't necessarily translate into buying behaviour. But, in this real-world case, it's notable that the older generation seems to be more politically motivated than the younger, and there is scepticism across the board when it comes to brands getting involved.

More recently, a November 2023 New York Times / Siena poll found that 46% of 18-29 year olds would vote for Trump if the election were held on that day, only one percentage point behind Biden.[26] A follow-up survey by NBC[27] found that Trump had pulled ahead in this age group by 46% to 42%. In each case, the results show not just a drifting away from Biden towards left-wing candidates, but a positive drift towards Trump.

Questioned on some of his sponsorship deals, basketball legend Michael Jordan once remarked "Republicans buy sneakers too." He later claimed to be half-joking, but he was also right. Judging by recent polls, it may be that Republicans are 46% of the Gen Z market. If nothing else, that's worth a brand pondering before it goes too deep into the politics it assumes people want reflected back at them.

Of course, polls are wayward and it's a time-honoured truth that younger people tend to lean more left than right. But it's hard to look at any of this evidence and see a generation unique in its political progressivism, clamouring for corporations to step up and take the lead. And, contrary to the report from Deloitte quoted above, it appears pay does matter a lot to younger people. The New York Times poll found 62% of 18-29 year olds rank economic issues, such as jobs, taxes and cost of living, as most important to them. Only 29% choose societal issues including abortion, guns and democracy.

All this boils down to three points. First, the politics of all generations are mixed, and have been broadly split down the middle on the big questions of the past decade. Second, the views of Gen Z are more complex and diverse than the whisperers would have marketers believe. Third, and most important for our purposes, none of it has much bearing on the brands we buy in any case.

Purpose builds on a weak foundation

We've already seen how 'starting with why' leads to sameness and abstraction, turning all brands into a slightly different version of 'We're here to make the world a better place'.

But it also brings to mind the politically-not-very-correct

joke about the traveller asking the way to Dublin, to which the Irish local replies "Well if I were you, I wouldn't start from here."

When a brand starts with why, it's the first branch on a decision tree that continues splitting in many directions before eventually materialising as an ad that appears in someone's living room. And some weird ads have been appearing lately.

Take the example of Hellmann's mayonnaise, part of the Unilever company. In 2019, Unilever CEO Alan Jope announced that "Brands without purpose will have no long-term future at Unilever."[28] His idea was that every brand at Unilever, from detergent to ice cream to fabric conditioner, should have a purposeful 'why'.

So began what we are obliged to call The Road to Hellmann's.

Hellmann's is a brand that has existed for over 110 years, but it only recently discovered that its true purpose is to reduce food waste—by helping to use up leftover food in your fridge. This repositioning came in for scathing criticism from Unilever investor Terry Smith, who said, "A company which feels it has to define the purpose of Hellmann's mayonnaise has, in our view, clearly lost the plot."[29]

For the moment at least, let's give the benefit of the doubt to the claim. It's not *totally* unbelievable to say Hellmann's could play a role in reducing food waste. If you have some eggs to use up, or some faded-looking salad, maybe you can liven it up by using some mayonnaise, thus rescuing food that would otherwise go to waste. Maybe?

Some might shrug and run with it. But I think most

punters will agree it's… a bit of a stretch. After all, you could equally argue that mayonnaise simply adds to food waste—another item gradually turning yellow in the back of your fridge. Maybe eggs are the real heroes in this, helping to use up your leftover Hellmann's.

But the point is that, by starting from a slightly stretched claim, you find yourself in a strange place. Having started with why, Hellmann's ended up with a surreal 2023 Super Bowl ad, in which actors Jon Hamm and Brie Larsson played the roles of ham and brie in Pete Davidson's fridge. A giant Pete Davidson stares at them hungrily while they stand next to a jar of Hellmann's discussing how they might make a good dinner combination. The endline is 'Make Taste Not Waste'.

There was a valiant attempt to do the whole thing with humour, but in the end I felt sorry for the creatives involved, because you're fundamentally starting from an overclaim and straining to make it work.

Of course, many brands start from an overclaim. We're the world's favourite airline (British Airways). We're probably the best lager in the world (Carlsberg). We give you wings (Red Bull). But it's one thing to exaggerate about your product; it's another thing to make an exaggerated moral or ethical claim—and that's what purpose tempts you to do. As viewers, we're supposed to find the pay-off persuasive. But when the pay-off is that Hellmann's helps to reduce food waste, it's natural to think 'Wait, say that again'. As the Terry Smith quote suggests, the idea of Hellmann's having a purpose is unintentionally funnier than anything in the ad itself.

Does this mean it's a bad ad that won't work? Well, to echo the Chinese premier who was asked in 1972 about the impact of the French Revolution… it's too early to say. One stubborn truth about advertising is that it's a cumulative process that builds across years and decades. Any Super Bowl ad is likely to be effective by virtue of being a Super Bowl ad. But the reason Hellmann's can afford that airtime is down to the decades of product-based advertising that got it into this market-dominant position. To that extent, all purpose ads stand on the shoulders of giants.

Meanwhile, behind all this humour lies some serious corporate manoeuvring. The pushback from Terry Smith was a sign of things shifting for Unilever. Another was the outbreak of war in Ukraine, which left some purposeful brands perilously exposed. Purely from a PR perspective, building your brand on a social purpose raises the stakes in these situations. We're used to hearing about businesses doing suspect, even scandalous, things. But when it's a company that claims moral superiority, it sets up a pride-before-fall narrative that the media can't resist—leading to a harsher backlash.

"Unilever named 'international sponsor of war' by Ukraine", said the Guardian headline in July 2023. A demonstration outside the Unilever headquarters included a bleak parody of a Dove poster, featuring five soldiers who had lost limbs and eyes. "Dove is owned by Unilever, which paid an estimated $331 million in taxes to Russia in 2022," said the caption.

Unilever claimed it had suspended all imports and exports of products into and out of Russia, and stopped all media and advertising spend. However, they continued to supply "everyday essential food and hygiene products made in Russia to people in the country". As the Wall Street Journal pointed out, Unilever was using an expansive definition of 'essential' that included ice cream, air fresheners and make-up brands like Little Fairy (Unilever's cosmetics brand for children).[30]

Danone, the 'enterprise à mission' mentioned earlier in our story, found itself in a similar scrape, given that 6% of its business relied on Russia. During a virtual tour with Western governments, Volodymyr Zelensky reserved particular ire for the French corporate sector, accusing it of financing "the murder and rape of women and children". Danone's CEO put out a defensive statement, saying: "It is very easy to get drawn into black-and-white thinking and demagogic positions, but in the end our reputation is about our behaviour."[31] Three years earlier, his predecessor Emmanuel Faber was urging brands to "Be bold or die."[32] If Danone was opposed to black-and-white thinking, it was a late convert.

All these rumblings, coupled with a bungled takeover attempt of rival GSK, contributed to a significant change in mood at Unilever. Having announced in 2019 that brands without purpose had no long-term future at the company, Alan Jope found his own future curtailed in 2023. His successor Hein Schumacher said purpose could be an "unwelcome distraction" that may have "diluted efforts" in areas like performance.[33]

It's worth mentioning one other structural weakness with purpose. Byron Sharp has suggested that it's too easy for more dominant brands to imitate. So even if advertisers are successful in persuading customers that their mayonnaise should contribute positively to society, a supermarket own-brand can fairly easily muscle in and announce it's giving 5% of sales to charity.

It's a rational criticism—but, so far, the signs may be pointing in the other direction. Supermarkets are no doubt spectating on stories like Unilever and Danone and deciding discretion is the better part of valour. After all, among other things, Unilever has been accused of price-hiking and profiteering during the economic downturn ("Nice profit margins, Unilever, but spare us the 'sharing the pain' gloss" said the Guardian in July 2023.) Most supermarkets will take note and prefer to change the subject.

Meanwhile, Hellmann's survived 110 years without a social purpose, and will survive long afterwards. I suspect Jon Hamm and Brie Larsson will be remembered as a weird cheese dream.

Purpose centres the brand, not the customer

Now the case for the prosecution comes to its key argument. Purpose makes everything about the brand, not the customer. And this is one of the cardinal sins of marketing.

One of my high points as a copywriter was appearing in The Copy Book: How Some of the Best Advertising Writers in the World Write Their Advertising (Taschen, 2018). Updated since its original 1995 edition, the book is a compendium of work by advertising copywriters, alongside short essays talking about their perspective and process. Many of the writers come from what is considered the golden age of advertising, from the 1960s through to the 1990s. There's David Abbott and his work for The Economist, Volvo and Sainsbury's; Indra Sinha and his work for the Metropolitan Police and Amnesty International; and Mary Wear for her work on London Underground and Make Poverty History. (There are also plenty of oversights, with a heavy leaning towards male writers in the original edition, albeit from class backgrounds that are more diverse than you might find today.)

Reading the contributions by each writer, you will notice a recurring theme. For people in the business of writing on behalf of brands, this is a rare chance to talk about themselves. But instead, they keep changing the subject to someone else: the reader.

Mary Wear says: "Know your target audience. Not intellectually, but intuitively. Think like them, empathise with them, identify with them." Steve Hayden says: "If you want to be a well-paid copywriter, please your client. If you want to be an award-winning copywriter, please yourself. If you want to be a great copywriter, please your reader." John Salmon says: "You should write from the standpoint of the reader's self-interest." Steve Harrison says: "Read your copy and check that 'you' appears three times more than 'I' or 'we'. This helps you write about the subject from the reader's perspective."

Later in this book, we'll explore the deeper idea of cognitive empathy that underlies all this. But for now, the point is straightforward: the secret to being a writer is to think about the reader. How are they likely to be feeling when they encounter this ad? How would you feel if you were them? What would make you read instead of turning the page? What objections are likely to be forming in their heads as they read this sentence? How can you answer them in the next one?

Purpose pushes you in the opposite direction. You may remember those purpose statements from a previous chapter: *We imagine a world where you can belong anywhere. We elevate the world's consciousness. We ignite opportunity by setting the world in motion. We give people the power to build community and bring the world closer together. We inspire and nurture the human spirit: one person, one cup and one neighborhood at a time. We unlock the potential of human creativity.*

One mention of 'you'. Lots of mentions of 'we'.

Maybe that's harsh—you might expect an internal purpose statement to be focused on 'we' more than 'you' (which is part of the problem with purpose statements). And don't some of the classic slogans, like 'Avis: We try harder', fall into that trap too?

True enough—you can't make all writing fit a simple paradigm. But what's undeniable about purpose is that it turns the perspective inwards. The advice to businesses is to look deep into yourself and work out what's really driving you. What do you stand for? What's getting you out of bed in the morning? What difference do you want to make in the world? As a result, the language is all: *We believe that... Our values are... We're leading the conversation about... We're starting a movement... We're here to make the world a better place.* Frequently, the language is all about origin stories too: *Our founders were sitting round the kitchen table when… Our founders were chatting in the pub when…*

All of it is an extended conversation that the brand conducts with itself, about itself. Readers outside the marketing industry might be surprised to hear quite how deep and involved these conversations are. Many a white board has borne the brunt of the purpose era. Circles have been drawn. Pillars of purpose, values and visions have been erected. PowerPoints have been pointed at. Many yellow stickies have fallen in combat, brushed aside by a new marketing manager with a slightly different vision for making the world a better place.

Some purpose advocates will object that purpose can still be about the customer: it's about living your values in a way that customers recognise and respect. But in reality, the brand is like the narcissist on a first date: "But enough about me. What do *you* think about me?" The act of listening to customers is predicated on the idea that the brand can play an important role in response. Even supposedly outward-looking purpose relies on an inflated vision of what brands are and the role they play in people's lives.

For a vivid demonstration of this, venture (carefully) onto what was called Twitter and is now X, then check the 'replies' timeline of any consumer brand. Throughout the era of purpose, which coincided with the rise of social media, there has been a fascinating dynamic where brands post visionary messages to the world about leading a movement and invite people to 'join the conversation'. But then their @ replies are a succession of apologies to customers making mundane complaints about a stale pack of crisps, a late delivery, or an undercooked burger.

It's a unique form of conversation. In one direction runs purpose and what brands like to think they are; in the other direction runs reality and what customers think brands are. I remember noticing this when Walker's Crisps, the UK's leading potato chip brand, put its name to a mental health awareness campaign. I took a screengrab at the time—here's a transcript of the timeline (with the user handles tweaked for discretion):

> Walkers Crisps: Being not fine is ok, we need to be able to talk about how we're feeling as the more we do it, the easier it gets
>
> Matt Black: @walkers_crisps Please don't tell me you've stopped making Sizzling Steak Wotsits?
>
> Matt Black: @walkers_crisps Beef and Onion… Sizzling Steak… what do you do for people who DO like those flavours?
>
> Walkers Crisps: @mattblack We're really sorry for the disappointment caused and we'll bear your feedback in mind.
>
> Walkers Crisps: Talking really is so important and like you say we need to do all we can to encourage people sharing how they're feeling #FineIsNotFine

It's not that Walkers is saying anything wrong—of course,

talking can be important for mental health. But the advice lands differently when it comes from your crisp supplier rather than your therapist, especially when it's punctuated by Matt and his sizzling steak issues, with which I relate.

At the time of writing, I've just been over to the Dove timeline and found another example, again with user handles changed:

Shay Thompson: Pleased to announce that I was part of the Dove 'Code My Crown' campaign, which is an extensive guide to creating Black hair in games. A lot of love went into creating the resource that comes with guides, reference pics and more.

Dove: @Shay_Thompson Say it with us: Representation matters

Ems: @dove hi, what's the best way to contact about a faulty product?

Dove: @ems Hi there! When you have a moment please send us a DM, so we can help.

Dove: 85% of Black gamers think video games poorly represent natural hair. Let's change that! It's time to level-up on Black hair representation in gaming. Click the link to learn more and download the guide!

FullyHilled: @dove you got some explaining to do giving my homeboy a chemical burn in his arm pits.

Dove: @fully_hilled We're so sorry to hear that. Please encourage your friend to reach out to us, so we can get more information to help!

You get the idea. While these are not entirely serious examples, they speak to a point about purpose that I think is fundamental. Having worked on the front line of branding for the past decade and more, I've seen many brands engaging in an extended exercise in earnest navel-gazing, instead of looking outwards to the world. As we'll see later, there is much to be gained from a radical perspective shift. It's not about your brand and its purpose; it's about the world outside. Whether you're selling deodorant, snacks or home insurance, there is a vast market out there, full of people who have purposes of their own.

Purpose might work internally. But in whose interest?

There are some purpose advocates who broadly accept all of the above, but retreat to a new holding position. Maybe purpose isn't great for external marketing, but it's a powerful internal attractor and motivator for employees, partners and suppliers. Having an inspiring, higher purpose must surely work at that level.

Some evidence has been brought forward for this—it tells a wider story, so it's worth a digression.

In 2021, marketing researcher Peter Field looked into the IPA Effectiveness Awards database—a bank of case studies entered into an advertising awards scheme based on measurable impact. His goal was to look at the impact of purpose-driven campaigns when compared to non-purpose-driven.[34]

There are some inbuilt issues with this. First, the IPA database is an unreliable data set, in that it consists of evidence prepared by the ad agencies themselves in order to win awards, based solely on the data that clients are willing to share. So it's not exactly a transparent window into the reality of how marketing works. Second, how are you defining a purpose-driven campaign? There's a lot of subjectivity in those calls (we've seen how slippery purpose can be as a term), and there's not much explication in Field's research about how the decisions were made.

Nevertheless, a clear result emerged. Out of the 333 non-purpose campaigns and 47 purpose campaigns, the purpose ones did much worse. According to the metric being used, the non-purpose campaigns generated 1.6 'very large' business effects, while purpose campaigns generated only 1.1. The difference of 45% is larger than even purpose sceptics might have expected.

The research could have stopped there, but didn't. In a move that he admitted would be criticised for 'sampling on the dependent variable', Peter Field stripped out the worst of the purpose-driven ads and kept the best-performing 27. Then, rather than comparing this high-performing group with a proportional high-performing group from the non-purpose ads (where, it later transpired, purpose would still have come out worse), he compared his best 27 with the whole of the non-purpose group. This comparison of 27 versus 333 ads eventually delivered the headline that the research seemed keen to create. The result was flipped: the purpose-driven ads won by 2.1 to 1.6. The subsequent press coverage was heavily slanted towards 'purpose works', with the less impressive details tucked deep in the paragraphs below.

I wrote about this at the time, because no one in the marketing press seemed to pick up on a crucial factor in the research: it had a sponsor. And it was our favourite enterprise à mission, Danone. All of this happened shortly after that story I mentioned in the introduction about their purposeful CEO Emmanuel Faber being elbowed out by impatient shareholders. Now Danone was forced into a position where it had to remake the case for purpose and its commercial effectiveness.

None of this is to suggest anything underhand by Peter Field, who was transparent about both the sponsor and the process. But it's not unreasonable to think Danone might have considered its sponsorship money badly spent if the initial result had been the sole outcome. The unusual methodology and subsequent positive headlines were more palatable.

I'm relating all of this because there was another finding in the Peter Field/IPA research: that purpose works particularly well as a motivator for employees, partners and suppliers.

It should already be clear that these insights aren't exactly rock-solid. Nevertheless, it's a reasonable proposition that people might prefer working for, or working with, companies that claim a higher purpose and a sense of making a difference to wider society.

The question is whether that's a good thing. We've already mentioned the Deloitte report suggesting Gen Z employees might be happier with lower salaries because it's more important for them to work somewhere meaningful. We should at least be alert to how this might be gamed by employers. If you're a big corporate, there are already ESG and BlackRock-driven incentives to embrace a purposeful agenda. But you might also see it as a useful way to appeal to bright, idealistic graduates. Some of them might be tempted by careers in NGOs, charities, schools or healthcare. The pay might be lower, but the work might be more fulfilling.

What if you could offer the best of both worlds? Become a management consultant, trainee marketer, or software engineer, and enjoy doing social good while doing well out of the private-sector benefits. And if it sometimes requires late nights or long weekends, don't obsess too much about money—remember you're on a social mission.

If that sounds cynical, it's worth reading some of the real-world stories about the cult-like working practices at purposeful WeWork, or at Daylight (the LGBTQ+ bank whose story you wouldn't believe if you saw it in a film).[35] But even in the less extreme cases, all this is a matter of systemic incentives, which push companies towards spinning a positive story in the hope of keeping up with the Dow Joneses.

"Purposeful Work: The Secret Weapon in the New War for Talent" says the headline on the Bain & Company website. "A war for climate talent is hotting up" says the Financial Times. "Employees Seek Personal Value and Purpose at Work. Be Prepared to Deliver." says Gartner.

Meanwhile, we see the rise of trends such as 'quiet quitting' and 'lazy girl jobs'—signs that Gen Z is detaching itself from the corporate purpose narrative. "Why not just focus on having an easy life, while finding meaning and life satisfaction outside of career stress?" says a report on so-called lazy girl jobs in the Guardian.[36] "Quiet quitting: why doing the bare minimum at work has gone global," says another report, quoting Maria Kordowicz, an associate professor in organisational behaviour at the University of Nottingham, who talks about how "people's relationship to their work has changed".[37] A Gallup poll finds only 9% of workers in the UK are engaged or enthusiastic about their work.[38] And the trend echoes what has been called the 'great resignation' in the US, owing to a general sense of burnout.

All this comes after several years in which employers have been actively pushing the idea of purpose as a way to appeal to employees. Maybe it helps on the cover of the graduate recruitment brochure and maybe it persuades more idealistic young people to apply. But might it also fuel the subsequent sense of disillusion and burnout? People aren't stupid. Even if they want to believe in the 'do well by doing good' narrative, many sense that it doesn't feel right on some level. Rather than feeling inspired, they feel subtly controlled. Toe the purposeful line and don't ask awkward questions or you'll be labelled a cynic—we need can-do people!

In some cases, it may work differently. If a wave of new employees joins on the basis of social purpose, they can reasonably feel entitled to bring their politics into the workplace and be vocal about cherished causes. Suddenly, the boss who talked passionately about changing society for the better is faced with a truculent workforce that wants to fire a fellow worker for having the wrong political opinions, or demands to stop using a long-term supplier because they rely too much on fossil fuels, or asks for paid leave to attend a political protest. When you've been telling a social purpose story, it's hard to know when the social purpose stops and the 'Can we just get on with work?' starts.

So yes, I can see how purpose might work as an internal motivator. If enough people believe in it for enough of the time, then it becomes self-fulfilling. But ground-level reality has a habit of catching up at some point, and we may already be seeing the effects in wider society. As we'll see later, that's no bad thing. If people start to think of purpose as something bigger than work, it can lead to a healthier and happier relationship with work itself.

Purposeful marketing is neither

Now for the closing argument, which I believe could stand on its own as a case against purpose, and which nods to the biblical quote at the start of this chapter.

Once you turn purpose into marketing, it stops being either

purpose or marketing. We've already seen how it weakens the marketing itself, turning it into an inward-looking, abstract exercise that tilts towards sameness, misunderstands how people buy things, builds on a weak foundation, centres the brand and not the customer, and becomes increasingly detached from reality.

But the more fundamental point is that it turns purpose into self-interest, in a way that stops it being purposeful. 'Do well by doing good' is the mantra from the point of view of the brand. But viewed from the outside, the question arises: If you're doing so well out of it, is it really doing good?

Writer and advertising planner Ian Leslie gave a talk about this in late 2017, in which he relates it to the idea of 'costly signalling'.[39] The classic example of costly signalling in nature is the peacock's tail—an elaborate signal of virility to impress any interested females. The tail apparently puzzled Darwin because he understood its purpose—mate selection—but didn't see why it had to be quite that over-the-top, to the point where it was a ridiculous weight for any bird to have to carry around.

The generally accepted theory now is that the over-the-topness is the point. The fact that carrying this plumage comes at such a large cost to the male is what makes it so impressive: the more excessive, the better.

Ian Leslie relates this to the early Quaker businesses in the UK—including Cadbury, Rowntree and Clarks—who operated on benevolent religious principles that extended to building entire towns to house workers in better conditions than they would otherwise enjoy. At the time, the point of this wasn't to feature it in a marketing campaign or make it part of an 'experiential' Cannes Lions entry. To the outside world, it was nevertheless a signal that Cadbury must be pretty successful if it could afford to do stuff like this. Like the peacock and its tail, the cost to the business was what made it impressive.

Ian Leslie's recommendation is that businesses should do one of two things. Most virtuously, they could do social good and not talk about it. Generally, this strikes us as morally admirable—there's nothing more impressive than hearing stories after someone's death about how kind and supportive they were to others, or how much good community work they did, without ever blowing their own trumpet. More humorously, this brings to mind the Curb Your Enthusiasm episode where Larry David gives an anonymous charitable donation, then subtly tries to spread the word that it was him, before eventually being reduced to screaming "I'm anonymous!" by the end of the episode.

Alternatively, Ian Leslie suggests brands could talk about doing good things, but make sure the story is about what this is costing you, not how well it's working for you. That's still a delicate thing to pull off—it could end up like someone giving money to a homeless person on the street, before grabbing a loud hailer and saying, "Look at that! 50 quid! Not sure how I'm going to eat tonight, but shucks, had to be done!"

But it's at least saner advice than the theory of purposeful marketing.

It's also rooted in the words of an adman whom I quoted in my first article about purpose back in 2017, and who provides the inspiration for the road away from hell.

"A principle isn't a principle until it costs you something," said Bill Bernbach in 1971.

For this chapter at least, the prosecution rests.

4.
How purpose leads to a worse world

Half the harm that is done in this world is due to people who want to feel important. They don't mean to do harm; but the harm does not interest them. Or they do not see it, or they justify it because they are absorbed in the endless struggle to think well of themselves.

– T.S. Eliot, *The Cocktail Party, 1949*

Early 2020s and you are walking to the corner shop.

You pass a poster with a vivid portrait of a Covid nurse who has just finished a harrowing twelve-hour shift. 'Courage is beautiful' says the headline, next to the Dove logo. You narrowly avoid a parcel being hurled into a hedgerow by a passing Amazon driver. The driver looks exhausted and you let it go. Crossing the road, weaving between Uber Eats drivers, you step over the stream from a burst Severn Trent water main and glance up at the HSBC billboard saying 'We are not an island'.

Inside the corner shop, a radio burbles about a tech founder beginning an eleven-year prison sentence. You pick up a paper, where the headline talks about the cost of living crisis. Scanning the shelf, you grab a four-pack of Bud Light, at which the shopkeeper makes an expression you can't quite interpret, then decide on a whim to buy a sharing-size bar of Dairy Milk for the walk back. Outside, you mumble an apology to the Big Issue seller, then flinch as a Volkswagen diesel car sails past, sending up a spray from the burst water main. Damp and demoralised, you wander home, half-waving as your neighbour's door opens, but it turns out to be out-of-towners who booked it on Airbnb.

You walk inside, turn on the TV and hear a voice saying, "For the ups and downs and everything in between. Halifax: It's a people thing." You crack open a can, stare out the window and ponder revolution.

***

If purposeful marketing doesn't work, why worry? Few

will shed a tear at Unilever or HSBC making a little less money. And surely we can rely on the market and restless shareholders to sort it out eventually?

As my tableau above is designed to suggest, it's not quite as simple as that. Like it or not, we all have to live in a world full of the background noise of purposeful brands. And it goes deeper. Purpose is more than a marketing idea: it's a theory of business that affects how corporations operate in the world. This surfaces in real-world consequences, whether it's Severn Trent Water sending confidential emails about embracing social purpose as a way to avoid regulation, or rising homelessness as banks post their highest profits since the 2008 crisis.[40]

This chapter examines the ways in which purpose, for all its professed good intentions, leads to worse social outcomes. Think of it as a map of the road to hell. And it starts where the last chapter left off.

Purpose leads to bad marketing

This is a bad thing in itself.

At its most basic level, marketing is socially useful. You don't have to be a free market radical to recognise that a new, independent pizza place down the road, upon whose fortunes a family's future depends, might benefit from designing a nice shopfront, posting some flyers, and booking a few Facebook ads. On a larger scale, you might look at companies like AstraZeneca, whose giant site near my home town of Macclesfield keeps 4,700 people gainfully employed and offers 160 apprenticeships every year. Those people in turn shop at Tesco, Morrisons and the local artisan deli, eat at the new independent pizza place, call out plumbers when their taps are dripping, pay their taxes, contribute to charities, bring up kids, look after elderly parents, and even buy the odd Patagonia fleece.

Advertising writer and adland critic Steve Harrison makes this point in his 2020 book Can't Sell, Won't Sell: "Every time someone buys something we've advertised, we enable someone else to get paid. And not just the person in the shop where it was purchased. That sale pays the wages of the person who made the thing. Or grew it. The person who packaged it. The person in the warehouse where it was stored. The person who delivered it to the shop. And the person who cleaned the shop after closing time."

Some will answer that it's naive to think markets work so benevolently—what about worker exploitation, tax dodging and squeezing suppliers? But it's equally naive to overlook the usefulness of markets when they function effectively—and certainly a strange position to take if you work in marketing.

All this means advertising has a valuable role to play during a cost of living crisis. Brands have a reactionary habit of slashing marketing spend in a recession, but research suggests it's the brands who maintain their spending that emerge stronger—not because they are trying to drive up short-term profits, but because they are laying the groundwork to capitalise on recovery.[41] By investing in brand advertising, you continue to build the long-term 'mental availability' that we discussed earlier, while your competitors are cutting back and losing ground.

If you were head of an advertising industry body, you might think there's a positive story to be told about all this. You could highlight the importance of the advertising industry to economic recovery, or talk about the power of creative thinking to drive commercial outcomes. Instead, the industry shop window at Cannes and D&AD remains full of ads that highlight social issues, ranging from suicide to transgenderism to school shootings. The commercial, populist stuff rarely gets a look-in when it comes to the top awards. Even then, it's a campaign featuring mouldy Whoppers, which seems likely to drive career-boosting attention to the marketing team, but less likely to drive punters to Burger King.[42]

If purpose leads to worse marketing, that's bad news for businesses and the people whose livelihoods depend on them. It's a simple point, but surprisingly controversial in a world where many people, even in marketing, have a vague instinct that degrowth is desirable for climate progress. In reality, that experiment has been tried on a colossal scale during the lockdown, when global GDP fell by three per cent. According to the World Bank, the pandemic cast nearly 70 million more people into extreme poverty, and left between five and seven million children struggling with pandemic-related malnutrition. All this reduced 2020 global carbon emissions by about six per cent. With 10 more years of global lockdown, we might get close to the Paris Climate Agreement targets, but only at the expense of enormous human misery and likely social collapse.[43]

Maybe you still back a post-capitalist future of degrowth, but there remains the stubborn question of democratic legitimacy—how will you persuade people to vote for it? At some level, it will involve communicating persuasive messages on a mass scale, and in some sense that will involve advertising, whether through conventional media or otherwise. Advertising serves many masters, from charities to social enterprises to political movements to corporations. "Everyone hates advertising until they lose their cat," said adman Dave Droga. You could go further: everyone hates advertising until they want to change the world.

Purpose is a pollutant

Advertising is part of a social contract that has evolved haphazardly over time. Flyposting was practised in Europe as early as the 15th century, but the first billboard only came along in 1835. It advertised a circus by Ringling Brothers and Barnum & Bailey—complete with their slogan 'The Greatest Show on Earth'. The sheer scale of the 50-foot hoarding would have been enough to guarantee attention, but creator Jared Bell nevertheless set out to deliver a work of commercial art, full of rich colours and vibrant characters. The poster, like most good advertising, was better than it strictly needed to be. And what drove Jared Bell, as with many creators, was a twofold desire: first to take pride in the craft, above and beyond the immediate need; and second, to fulfil his side of the unspoken social contract. If we're going to take over the public realm like this, there's a responsibility to make it halfway decent.

Advertising has consistently failed to live up to that promise ever since. But it has tried and often succeeded. If we're beaming into your living rooms to interrupt Coronation Street, we'd better do a JR Hartley ad (the legendary UK campaign for Yellow Pages), or a Smash Martians (the late 1970s campaign for instant mashed potato, which became more popular than many of the programmes it interrupted), or a bunch of dudes saying Whassup? (the 1999 Budweiser campaign that created a meme before we called them memes). Equally, if we're going to put giant billboards on every street corner, we should do a "66 was a great year for English football. Eric was born" (the 1996 Nike poster featuring Eric Cantona), or an "'I never read the Economist.' Management trainee. Aged 42" (the 1989 ad for The Economist). And if we're inserting ourselves into your newspapers, we should do a Lemon (the 1960 ad for the Volkswagen Beetle) or an "Ends Fri" (the 2004 ad promoting the last ever episode of Friends—note the elegant rearranging of the programme title).

At their best, ads become more than ads. They exist primarily as commercial creations, to fulfil a specific goal at a specific time. But they can take on a life of their own, as cultural artefacts that outlast the brands and people who commissioned them. Many Britons of a certain age will remember JR Hartley and the Smash Martians; few will have used Yellow Pages or Smash in years.

All this is to say that advertising should try to be good.

You're like an uninvited house guest: if you're sufficiently funny, charming or good-looking, the owner might not mind too much. Legendary adman David Ogilvy started out as a door-to-door salesman and learned how to relate to the person in front of him. Most of the time, you're a nuisance, but on a good day you might talk someone round to buying something they'll appreciate.

Now advertising is more like a Jehovah's Witness, knocking on your door to ask if you've thought about Purpose lately. Most brands preach with the zeal of the recent convert: we've just discovered climate change / transgenderism / Pride marches / menstruation / mental health—would you like to join our conversation about it? Commercial breaks and billboards are full of brands casting themselves as the heroes in their own narratives, and inviting people to ride with them into the sunset.

This chapter will go on to discuss more substantive arguments against purpose, but I attach some importance to this one, which is more subtle but all-pervasive. Purpose is partly a question of taste. There is something demoralising about walking around in a culture where billboards contain pictures of exhausted Covid nurses staring down at you, not with a message saying 'support this charity' or 'become a nurse', but with a slogan linking it to the ongoing brand campaign by Dove. I suspect most people respond to it well enough, including the nurses featured—because it is moving and inspiring to celebrate these people in public spaces. But we have become accustomed to the idea that messages like these must always come with a commercial pay-off attached. 'Courage is beautiful' is the price we pay for celebrating the nurses: now go buy your deodorant.

Elsewhere, an emotional film comes on during an ad break, portraying the life of an autistic girl and her family, all of whom are admirably played by a real-life family. The story opens with the girl's mother struggling to get her out of bed on a school morning. We wonder what's coming. The story continues with the girl donning her school uniform and black hoodie. We start to feel it coming. Stressed and socially confused at school, the girl retreats into a sensory room and hides beneath her hoodie. We feel it getting closer. Back home, Dad is doing the laundry and a product shot appears in the foreground. It's definitely coming. Now the sister of the autistic girl has stolen her hoodie and the mother is struggling to contain a meltdown. Soon the hoodie reappears with apologies and hugs. 'Autistic girls are 3 times less likely to receive a diagnosis than boys' says the advert, correctly, but having just portrayed a girl who is unambiguously autistic and receiving help accordingly. In some parallel world, that line might have been the pay-off, with an Ambitious About Autism logo and a fundraising number. But we know the real pay-off is still coming. And now it appears: the Vanish logo, with the line 'Making clothes live longer really matters'. Thanks to Dad using Vanish, the hoodie is still in wearable condition, which matters greatly to this girl. Many parents of autistic children will nod in recognition, while also wondering about the wisdom of switching brands of fabric conditioner when dealing with highly sensory children.

Titled 'Me, My Autism and I', the film was made in response to a Channel 4 competition to promote diversity in advertising, with a prize on offer of £1m in airtime. The result is a worthwhile film, but an awkward ad, in which the most forced element is the link to the product. Brands aren't supposed to feel like impostors in their own ads, but very often that's where purpose pushes them. Like the Dove logo on the nurse's photo, it's a sign of the new social contract: we'll tell you purposeful stories, but you know the money shot is coming. And there it is, the Vanish logo at the top of the endframe, with the logo of Ambitious About Autism (a vital partner in the endeavour) demoted to second billing. Finally, there is the web address to find out more about autism—not via the charity, but via the commercial partner: vanish.co.uk/autism

There is a nuance to all this. Brands can and do play a deep role in people's lives. In 2014, the British press reported on a woman who had recently died and requested to be buried in a coffin branded in the colours and logo of Costa Coffee.[44] Inevitably, Costa Coffin took on a viral quality, but it was also a genuine human story. This woman really did like meeting her friends at Costa, and saw it as a consoling highlight of her later years. So yes, it's funny, but it's also real and true. What it isn't is an ad. As soon as you turn it into an ad, the real and true thing becomes a crass and insensitive thing. Because making something an ad changes what it is. Attaching a sales message to something changes what it is.

Intentionally or not, the brand purpose movement pushes the opposite idea. The central mantra is that 'Doing good is good business'. It actively encourages brands to harness social issues as a way of increasing sales. It flatters them into thinking they have a higher purpose beyond profit, when they usually don't.

As noted previously, Bill Bernbach said that a principle isn't a principle until it costs you something. Today's advertisers have turned that around—now it isn't a principle until it makes you money. Costa may have become an intensely meaningful part of some customers' lives as a byproduct of doing what it does, but that's not its purpose. Its purpose is to make money by selling coffee in nice places. That's why the woman liked it. If she'd been assailed on every visit by tear-jerking messages about how Costa is a deeply meaningful part of every customer's journey through life and death, she'd probably have gone to Caffè Nero.[45]

We'll return to this point later in the book, but for now let's note this wider effect of purpose as a pollutant in the information environment. Unlike some marketing commentators, I would be more worried if purpose *did* work well as a marketing device—because the last thing we need is more of it. In countless, low-level, inescapable ways, purpose keeps pushing this idea that social good must be allied to commercial gain. The latter is the price we pay for the former. Even if it works for the brands in question, what does it do to the rest of us? I think it has a demoralising effect: a sense of living in a world that's grubbier and more compromised than it really has to be, and a sense that political progress will always be the support act in the commercial circus.

Purpose fuels social division

"What's great about this country is America started the tradition where the richest consumers buy essentially the same things as the poorest. You can be watching TV and see Coca-Cola, and you can know that the President drinks Coke, Liz Taylor drinks Coke, and just think, you can drink Coke, too. A Coke is a Coke and no amount of money can get you a better Coke than the one the bum on the corner is drinking. All the Cokes are the same and all the Cokes are good."

When Andy Warhol wrote that in 1975, he was pointing to a useful role that mass market brands can play in culture: acting as a form of common ground. Four decades later, America would be torn apart by the rise of Diet Coke-loving Donald Trump, and many would bemoan the polarisation that appeared to push Democrats and Republicans into parallel versions of reality, much like Leavers and Remainers in the UK.

In such times, a brand like Coke can live up to its promise of being 'the real thing'—an aspect of shared reality upon which all Americans agree. Many brands are in a position to do this: we may have our differences, but in the end we can all enjoy a Bud, share a bag of M&Ms, kick back and watch a Disney movie. These are common reference points amid the maelstrom.

That's not the way it has panned out.

On 23 March 2023, marketing manager Alissa Heinerscheid appeared on the Make Yourself At Home podcast to talk about her new role as VP of Marketing at Bud Light—the first woman to hold the role in the brand's 41-year history.

It's clear from the interview that she saw her new post in highly personal and value-laden terms: "It just doesn't mean anything unless I am positively impacting other people and that's been just incredibly important to me... I try to bet on people with similar values as me, who are hungry and want to do great things, but also care about each other and protect each other and are kind and good."

She goes on to describe beer as a "vice industry" and says her mission is to turn around a brand in decline: "We have this hangover. I mean, Bud Light had been a brand of fratty, out-of-touch humour, and it was really important that we had another approach." As she saw it, the way forward was to attract younger drinkers: "So I had a super-clear mandate. We needed to evolve and elevate this incredibly iconic brand. And what I brought to that was a belief in... ok, what does evolve and elevate mean? It means inclusivity. It means shifting the tone. It means having a campaign that's truly inclusive and feels lighter and brighter and different, and appeals to women and to men. And representation is at the heart of evolution."

A month later, Alissa Heinerscheid was placed on an indefinite leave of absence, along with her boss Daniel Blake. In one of the wilder episodes in the culture wars, an almighty battle had broken out over the use of transgender Tik Tok influencer Dylan Mulvaney in a paid celebrity endorsement spot—part of Heinerscheid's inclusivity mission. Fuelled by musician Kid Rock posting a video of himself firing rounds into a stack of Bud Light cases, the backlash became a highly energised cause on the right-wing side of the culture wars. As they saw it, it was about reclaiming a brand that had shown contempt for its historic customer base in an attempt to woo a new (here comes the word) 'woke' generation. What looked like an overheated social media story ended up having real and sustained commercial results. Bud Light sales fell by 26% in the following months, parent company AB InBev's stock price fell 20%, and Bud Light lost its status as the top-selling beer in the United States to Modelo Especial, a spot it had held for 20 years. Even six months later, sales were reportedly down 30% and the story looks like becoming part of the permanent folklore of the brand.[46]

A separate book could be written about the cultural, political, commercial, technological and ethical currents that cascade into the whirlpool of a story like this. Some see it as a simple tale of inclusivity facing a bigoted backlash, where the marketing manager is the hero. By this reading, it's no different to the first inclusion of a gay couple in an ad, or the gradual reduction in sexist stereotypes that has taken place over the years. And it's true that adland can play a valuable role on this front. What looks like box-ticking to some can be genuinely heartening if you're a gay person seeing a same-sex embrace in a mainstream ad for the first time, or a woman seeing women cast as the CEO rather than the PA. As usual, brands approach these issues clumsily, but the Dylan Mulvaney move can be placed in that well-meaning tradition of tolerance and gradual changing of norms.

Others see the analogy as misplaced, as transgender rights exist as part of a wider ideology of gender that runs the spectrum from reasonable to radical, and comes into tension with the rights of other groups, including women and children. For the purposes of this chapter, it's not necessary to take a position on any of that. The point is that, right now, the job of a marketing manager or ad agency is to act as a smart and empathic navigator of culture, guiding their brand through or around the sensitive issues. And that works best when marketing managers are in a mindset of looking outwards, rather than inwards. It means recognising that the brand isn't an expression of your values or personal story arc, but is more like a container for the values of many people, who were all there long before you were. While there were some core elements of anti-trans bigotry, the wider Bud Light backlash was kicking back against a sense of being controlled and patronised. The audience knows the trans issue is wrapped up in a wider political world view with which they don't agree, and it doesn't help when marketing managers give highly personal interviews about the values they bring to the work.

As with Bud Light, so with M&Ms, who went through an elaborate exercise of introducing more "nuanced personalities" to their brand mascots. So the red one would become less confrontational and more kind, the orange one would "embrace his true self, worries and all", the green one would swap her go-go boots for sneakers to reflect "confidence and empowerment, as a strong female" and the brown one would swap her stilettos for pumps to become more of a "boss". The whole story was melodramatically weaponised by Tucker Carlson—part of a familiar culture wars dynamic where the initial incident is blown up into a confected outrage, which in turn is blown up into an excessive counter-reaction, then an excessive counter-reaction to the counter-reaction, then a wave of urgent think pieces about what it all means. Eventually, M&Ms announced they were putting the characters on "indefinite pause", saying the controversy was "the last thing M&Ms wanted since we're all about bringing people together".

There's a pantomime element to these stories—a sense that none of the players involved is deeply serious. But there's a reason they happen now as opposed to any other time, and it's not just that Tucker Carlson is randomly casting around for material. Consider the official statement when the M&Ms characters were launched: "At Mars we believe that in the world we want tomorrow, society is inclusive. And, as one of our most iconic brands, M&Ms is announcing a new global commitment to create a world where everyone feels they belong." It's the kind of grandiose statement that might have appeared preposterous 20 years ago, and should feel preposterous now. But in the age of purpose, it's routine. It comes from this sense that a brand—even a candy brand—needs to have a deeper sense of what it wants to achieve in society. And societal change will always be a contested area. Brands aren't the hapless victims of a culture wars attack that appeared out of nowhere. They're starting with why and ending with apology statements as they desperately scramble out of the quagmire and back towards common ground.

Disney has gone through a similar story arc in its battles with Republican governor Ron DeSantis. It started with the Disney Corporation's vocal opposition to Florida's Parental Rights in Education act, branded by critics as the Don't Say Gay bill. In retaliation at what he described as "woke corporations… peddling their unchecked pressure campaigns," DeSantis announced the state would be stripping

Disney of its special tax status—an expansive agreement secured by the Reedy Creek Improvement District, founded by Walt Disney, which afforded Disney the right to manage its own infrastructure, construction, utilities and fire station. The confrontation escalated into an ongoing legal battle, with Disney suing the governor, while also pulling the plug on a $1 billion office development project in the state.

Behind the headlines lies a tangled story about corporate power, state power, and the free speech rights of corporations. Richard Foglesong, political scientist and author of Married to the Mouse: Walt Disney World and Orlando (2001) has described Disney as a "state within a state", whose original charter has been used to avoid paying taxes ever since. One example was a tax that Orange County officials introduced in the 1990s to help cover the budget of its sheriff's department. Disney argued that it didn't apply to them because the charter protected it "in perpetuity" from paying any taxes adopted after 1967.

Foglesong doesn't endorse the attacks by DeSantis: "Disney's powers need to be addressed, but he's attacking the company for all the wrong reasons." But it's not as if there's nothing there to be attacked. And there are deeper issues about the political speech rights of corporations. Historically, you might expect Republicans to be pro-business and anti-regulation: let them say what they like and the market will decide. On the other hand, you might expect Democrats to be more concerned with the rights of individuals over corporations: how many of the 225,000 Disney employees are Republican supporters? What are they to do if their employer is speaking on their behalf, adopting political stances with which they don't agree? After all, corporate politics don't always align with majority opinion. In 2020, Facebook, Twitter and most of Silicon Valley got behind the Prop 16 vote on reinstating affirmative action in California.[47] The broadly left-leaning public disagreed by an increased majority that cut across ethnic divides. Some of those voters probably worked at Facebook and Twitter and kept quiet as their bosses issued confident statements on their behalf.

For now, the point is that corporate purpose pushes brands into adopting partisan positions that wind up being dangerous for the brand and unhelpful for society. From the point of view of the consumer, brands can be common ground on which Republicans and Democrats meet. From the point of view of the employee, corporations can be common ground where you rub shoulders with people from all parts of the political spectrum. The expansion of corporate purpose has shrunk the common ground just when it's needed most. Warhol said that a Coke is a Coke whether you're president or a bum. Now your choice of soft drink, candy brand or movie franchise says something about your place on the political spectrum. Social purpose fuels social division.

Purpose is tone deaf at social change

Sources dispute whether the year was 1975 or 1976, but they all place a graphic designer in the back of a New York cab, looking out at a city on the verge of bankruptcy, with crime rates soaring to an all-time high, and the population simmering with discontent that would soon escalate into rioting and looting. Born in the South Bronx to Hungarian Jewish immigrant parents, Milton Glaser, the designer in the back of the cab, had made his way into the world of commercial art and was now pondering a brief to design a logo for a New York tourism campaign. Scribbling in red crayon on a brown envelope, he drew a simple heart shape and arranged the letters I and NY around it. He would later say the cab driver made more money from that ride than he did.

I Heart NY remains one of the most recognisable graphic symbols in the world, launched in 1977 and taken to heart by a city that had reached rock bottom and was now ready to rise again. The early use of what was effectively an emoji spoke to something both hip and primal about the city: a brisk shorthand that communicated a lot with a little. When 9/11 came, Milton Glaser adapted the symbol to include a bruise on the heart and an extended slogan: 'I heart NY more than ever'. Other than that temporary shift, the symbol remained unchanged and as recognisable as the Statue of Liberty or the yellow cab.

In 2022, another graphic designer was commissioned to reconsider the logo. The approach came from MaryamB—"a purpose-driven collective with its sights set on New York City". That's the description on the agency's home page, which continues: "We are a group of passionate executives, entrepreneurs, creatives, dreamers and doers who mobilize groups and organizations around a purpose." The group's goal was to rally to the aid of New York City, which was now facing a new kind of challenge: recovering from a global pandemic. Graham Clifford, the graphic designer, came up with a symbol that was launched with fanfare in March 2023. A variation on Glaser's classic mark, the new logo added a rounded depth to the red heart, tweaked the 'NY' to 'NYC', and swapped the 'I' for 'We'.

The creators claimed this new We Heart NYC symbol wasn't designed to replace Milton Glaser's mark, but to update it for the modern era. "This was a time for 'we', not 'me'," explained Kathryn Wylde, president of the Partnership for New York City. "The message is, 'This takes all of us.'"[48]

The campaign met with near-universal derision. Comments on Twitter included: "The original looks like the voice of a city. The new one looks like the voice of an investment bank or possibly a healthcare provider." Another said: "This sucks on every conceivable level and also on some levels that exist beyond human perception." Adam Gopnik wrote an extended lament in the New Yorker,[49] the New York Times ran a series of negative reactions under the headline "These New Yorkers don't heart the We Heart NYC logo"[50] and the Washington Post relished reporting on the reaction with the headline: "New Yorkers bond over new city logo: They hate it."[51]

I have sympathy for the designer involved. The new logo appears to be the product of a 'multiple stakeholder' process involving the purpose-driven agency mentioned above and various city authorities and corporate partners. You can almost hear the fifteenth person in the room saying "Actually, it should be NYC not NY, to distinguish us from the state," or the murmured suggestions of making the heart 'pop' a little more (losing all the sense of casual speed that worked so well in the original). And you can definitely imagine the nods and quiet air punches when someone said "'We heart' is actually much better than 'I heart' because it's more inclusive and diverse isn't it? There's no I in Team!"

A recurring characteristic of Purpose is that it loves talking about 'We'. Sometimes it's writ large in the brand name: WeWork. Usually, it's a top-down 'We' imposed by a distant, disembodied corporation: "We are not an island" says the HSBC campaign, beaming into the high streets of Birmingham, Liverpool and Manchester to tell the post-Brexit public that 'we' are all part of something much, much bigger.

Purpose believes 'we' is better than 'I', because 'I' is one person and that sounds selfish and limited, doesn't it? 'We' is more than one person, so it has to be more inclusive and empowering.

Milton Glaser instinctively knew this isn't how it works. The beauty of 'I heart NY' is that it's opt-in. Wear the badge or t-shirt if you want, but no one is forcing you into it, or assuming your agreement. People generally don't like feeling controlled or cajoled—and New Yorkers especially don't like it. As Dustin Hoffman shouts to the cab driver while crossing the street with Jon Voight in the film Midnight Cowboy: "Up yours, you son of a bitch, *I'm* walking here."[52]

The result was that I Heart NY became a collective symbol: something that locals and tourists were happy to buy into. It created a big, unspoken 'We' by not being literal about it. That's where the skills of creative marketers can be helpful. If you want to change human behaviour, it helps to understand human nature. Purpose starts from the assumption that it is right, and that its truths are self-evident. It's a closed way of thinking that conscripts everyone into this big blob of 'We'. It's tin-eared when it comes to actual social change.

The controlling tone of 'We' came out in the sniffy reaction to the social media backlash. "We heart critics," said a follow-up poster, "even if they don't like our new logo". The accompanying social media post said: "Now that we have your attention, it's up to US to take action."

That shouted 'US' is supposedly a rallying cry. Purpose stands like a teacher in front of an unruly class, saying "Well, I'm glad we're listening at least! Perhaps we would like to turn some of our reaction into doing something constructive, shall we? Have we thought about that?"

Once your campaign is in this position of expressing veiled disappointment in its audience, it's not a sign that things are going well. And that should be a relief to everyone, considering the expressed aims of a campaign sponsored by BlackRock, Amazon, McKinsey, Edelman, Facebook and others. Kathryn Wylde told the New York Times that the campaign was meant to "cut through divisiveness and negativity" and remind people that "we don't have to maintain these divisions that have grown up between business and labour and rich and poor".

Don't we? Are New Yorkers truly keen to overcome divisions between rich and poor, or business and workers, as Kathryn Wylde claims? Or are they keen to do the opposite: bust through the cosy 'we' that purpose imposes, and talk about how the rich have priced New Yorkers out of their own city, and corporate interests have diverted the economic anger of Occupy Wall Street into a decade of handwaving about social purpose instead?

All questions we'll explore later. Sorry, *I'll* explore later. Keep reading if you want.

Purpose leads to noble cause corruption

In September 2009, as the purpose era was taking hold, Silicon Valley founder Elizabeth Holmes welcomed Ramesh 'Sunny' Balwani to the board of her startup, Theranos. The company was developing a finger-prick blood testing device intended to diagnose patients for hundreds of conditions, including cancer and diabetes, using just a few drops of blood. The name came from a combination of 'therapy' and 'diagnosis'. Funding to the tune of $945 million came from investors including Rupert Murdoch, Henry Kissinger, former US Secretary of State George Shultz, and Betsy DeVos, Secretary of Education in the Trump administration. All were beguiled by the charisma of Holmes, a precocious Stanford University dropout who adopted a Steve Jobs-ian black polo neck, and affected a deep, slow speaking style that matched the gravity of her ambition. By 2014, Holmes was celebrated on the cover of Forbes magazine and hailed as the first female self-made billionaire, heading a company valued at $9 billion.

By 2023, she was beginning an 11-year jail sentence, while her colleague and former romantic partner Sunny Balwani faced 12 years.

The fall from grace was one of the bleaker parables of the purpose era. It turned out this secretive company was built on a pyramid of deceptions, wishful thinking, PR bluster, bullying management, and outright malpractice, all of which had shocking consequences for patients, some of whom were falsely told they had serious medical conditions, or falsely found to be in the clear. The deception eventually caught up with Elizabeth Holmes, who was found guilty of two counts of wire fraud and two counts of attempted wire fraud.

The story is told in Bad Blood by John Carreyrou, the journalist who dug through layers of resistance at Theranos and eventually got to the truth. The first chapter in his tale is titled 'A Purposeful Life' and it's clear that he sees Holmes's obsession with purpose as being central to her story. In a 2018 appearance on Stay Tuned, the podcast hosted by Preet Bharara, Carreyrou frames Holmes's downfall as an example of what he calls 'noble cause corruption'.

"[Elizabeth Holmes] felt strongly that the cause that she was pursuing was a noble one. Therefore all the cheating along the way to get there was perfectly justifiable because the cause was so noble."

The term 'noble cause corruption' was coined in 1989 by Edwin Delattre, professor of philosophy at Boston University. He used it to describe cases of police corruption where officers cut corners in service of what they see as the greater good. But it has come to describe any system of so-called 'teleological' ethics, where the end (telos) is used to justify the means. Purpose is a teleological system of ethics applied to corporations. By focusing on a distant north star, they are able to justify trampling over any norms and expectations that stand in their way. Elizabeth Holmes was convinced of her destiny, and saw every decision and micro-decision in the context of that larger narrative. The true narrative ended in a Texan prison cell.

Some might feel 'noble cause corruption' is too generous a description. For many patients, investors and mistreated employees, there is nothing noble in the Theranos story. To them, Holmes is a sociopathic narcissist whose talk of purpose was always a shallow cover story for the raw pursuit of money and power. But to others, including at least one member of the jury that convicted her,[53] Holmes seems, at least on some level, to have believed in the cause she espoused.

The story has since been adapted into a TV drama, and the motives of Holmes are a key part of the psychodrama. What's really going on inside her head? Does this driving belief that she will one day change the world blind her to the corners she is cutting? If so, is it truly a belief in the cause, or are those dollar signs she is seeing? Or is it a mix of both, with the occasional glimpse of self-awareness at the heart of it all? The evidence against Holmes includes an intriguing note she scribbled to herself as the walls were closing in. In it, she appears to compare herself to Bernie Madoff—the fraudster who ran the largest Ponzi scheme in history, back in the days when fraudsters knew they were fraudsters.

Either way, noble cause corruption is a useful descriptor for the psychology of Silicon Valley, with its presiding culture of 'Fake it until you make it'. Once you're convinced of the rightness of your cause, it's easier—consciously or subconsciously—to justify any means towards that end. And right now a lot of companies—whether cynically, genuinely, or somewhere in between—are convincing themselves of the rightness of their cause. What's more, they're being encouraged to do so by people in the advertising and branding industries, who whisper flatteringly in the ears of ambitious founders and their marketing teams.

Or maybe that's unfair to ad agencies. John Carreyrou's book includes a chapter on TBWA\Chiat\Day, the agency that worked with Theranos. For once, the ad people come out of it well. The more senior directors were understandably keen to court this female Steve Jobs who was on all the magazine covers. But the creative team got first-hand insight into the lack of substance behind the claims, at one point drawing up a spreadsheet to fact-check the assertions being made. It's distressing to read about one of the senior copywriters becoming so concerned about the misleading nature of the material, and so dismayed by the unreasonable demands of the client, that he suffered anxiety attacks and had to withdraw from the project. Within Theranos itself, there was the even worse case of a senior biochemist who took his own life, after becoming concerned about his role in the deception.

At the time, anyone raising questions could easily be cast as a naysayer whose pedantic concerns were getting in the way of the noble mission. If purpose is the culprit in all this, then positivity is its accomplice. The mantle of sunny optimist is often assumed as a pre-emptive move to close down criticism: "Look at me talking about changing society for the better, and all you can do is carp from the sidelines!" We saw it with Simon Sinek, whose LinkedIn page describes him as 'Author and Founder of The Optimism Company'. His bio opens: "Simon Sinek is an unshakeable optimist who believes in a bright future and our ability to build it together." Once you brand yourself as an optimist with a noble cause, any questioning can quickly be cast as negative and unhelpful.

Sinek's 'start with why' philosophy served Elizabeth Holmes well. As scepticism from journalists and investors mounted, it was the what, how, when and where questions that proved most awkward. What is the current balance sheet? How exactly does the device work? When will it be released? Where is the laboratory—can we see it? But ask Elizabeth Holmes why and she would be in her element, talking for hours about changing the world, transforming lives, helping American troops on the battlefield, helping doctors at home. She might air her anecdote about her uncle who died of skin cancer that might have been diagnosed sooner—the story that she says inspired her to follow this path. (It later transpired this uncle, to whom she wasn't especially close, died years after she founded her business.) But to whatever extent it's true or post-rationalised, this is the conversational comfort zone for Holmes. Through a combination of grand vision and personal founding myth, she could hold any audience spellbound.

A similar dynamic played out in the rise and fall of WeWork, whose founder Adam Neumann couched his business ambitions in the language of a transcendent social movement designed to 'elevate the world's consciousness'. Alongside his wife Rebekah (cousin of Gwyneth Paltrow), Neumann appointed himself the figurehead of what he called the 'We Generation' (another example of purpose's favourite pronoun)—all while funding an extraordinary alcohol and drug-fuelled lifestyle for himself. Propelled into the stratosphere by venture capital from Saudi Arabia and elsewhere, WeWork eventually came crashing to earth when its IPO exposed basic truths about the balance sheet that had been hidden under layers of wildly optimistic story-telling and semi-religious fervour.

The story is told in The Cult of We, by Eliot Brown and Maureen Farrell. In one key scene, Israeli-born Adam Neumann and his Chief Legal Officer Jennifer Berrent have just sealed a staggering deal for $4.4 billion in venture capital, and are belatedly pondering the geopolitical implications of taking money from Saudi Arabia and the UAE. "We're taking toxic money," says Neumann with what appears to be a genuine pang of conscience. Jennifer Berrent's reply is revealing: "I'm Jewish and gay... I'm not accepted in several different ways by the Saudi government—and many other groups of people. Let's take their money and do something good with it."

It's an example of noble cause corruption in action. Once you've convinced yourself that your end is noble, any means towards that end can be justified. After all, the investment will help WeWork in its noble mission to remake society by renting out flexible workspaces with nice coffee.

There's another telling detail in the book. We learn that Adam Neumann's office at WeWork's headquarters in Manhattan is in the same building where Oliver Stone filmed Wall Street back in the 1980s. Neumann's mantras of 'Do what you love' and 'Make a life, not just a living' were born just down the corridor from the office where Gordon Gekko memorably proclaimed 'Greed is good'. And it was more than a coincidence. Having looked into it further, I discovered Neumann and his co-founder Miguel McKelvey initially bonded over a shared love of the film.[54]

It's a poetic illustration of a real point. Instead of fearing a Gordon Gekko of tomorrow, we should fear the Gordon Gekkos of today: the ones in black polo necks or casual t-shirts, not pinstripes and braces. They are the most effective kind of con artist, because their first victims are themselves. Neumann's riches and hedonistic lifestyle weren't something he pursued secretly behind a purpose-wash cover story. He did it openly, because there is no contradiction in his philosophy. If your cause is noble and every time your valuation grows it furthers that cause, then greed really is good. Even better, it's not greed at all. You get to be a saint as well as a billionaire. Purpose and profit are two sides of the same infinitely valuable coin.

"Companies over countries," said another successful founder, Mark Zuckerberg, to his former speechwriter Kate Losse. He continued: "If you want to change the world, the best thing to do is to build a company." Losse subsequently described how the internal culture of Facebook was beset by endemic noble cause corruption. "Because to Facebook, growth is an ethical goal unto itself. When Facebook's technical mission to connect people is imagined as itself a moral good, all efforts in that direction become righteous by definition."[55]

From Zuckerberg to Neumann and Holmes, purpose renders business owners and employees vulnerable to this form of self-deception. The cynical reading is that businesses wear purpose as a "cloak of social responsibility"—to use Milton

Friedman's phrase. But the cloak also hides the business from itself, confusing board members and employees about their true incentives and responsibilities. Writing about the travails of Uber, Canadian journalist Cory Doctorow talks about the emperor's-new-clothes dimension to the story: "All of this is exactly what anyone with a shred of critical reasoning would have foretold from the very early days of Uber, but the company has managed to put up a surprisingly durable reality distortion field that kept the investments pouring in."[56]

Purpose is the reality distortion field. And founders and employees are as susceptible to it as anyone else. Once you convince yourself that Facebook exists to "bring the world closer together", or that Unilever exists "to make sustainable living commonplace", you start to see your company as a moral actor whose success has intrinsic value, rather than a profit-driven enterprise for which law and ethics should be a constraint, not an opportunity. Noble cause corruption is the pathology of the purpose movement. The road to hell starts in the mind.

Purpose undermines the public and not-for-profit sectors

This next part is more than a subsection—it's really the macro-argument of this whole book.

To bring the point to life, I want to focus on a specific case. I've chosen it not because it's a Pepsi-style example of obviously terrible advertising, but because it's one of the strongest examples on the purpose side of the debate.

In 2022, Cadbury won the 'social purpose' category and Best in Show at the IPA Effectiveness Awards, considered one of the more rigorous tests of whether a marketing campaign has had an impact in the real world. As we've seen in an earlier section on Peter Field and Danone, the IPA Effectiveness awards make for a strange dataset, consisting of papers prepared by ad agencies in order to win awards, using only the figures that clients are willing to share. Nevertheless, it introduces some semblance of objectivity by relating ads to their commercial results.

At least, that was the case until 2022, when the IPA began to shift its criteria. In the age of purpose, it no longer felt sufficiently inspiring to focus solely on commercial return-on-investment. Instead, the language around "financial returns" was shifted to the vaguer "value creation", with an invitation to entrants "to present evidence of value creation with reference to purely financial value, to societal or environmental value, or any combination of these".[57] At the same time, a new 'social purpose' category was introduced, specifically to honour this type of work. In other words, faced with a lack of purposeful work meeting its historic criteria, the awards body changed the criteria. If you can say it made a societal difference, maybe by 'raising awareness' of an important issue, then that would be enough to compete alongside the commercial entrants.

Cadbury duly entered the social purpose category, won, and went on to win Best in Show, allowing the IPA to be associated with a feel-good story about purpose, rather than an uninspiring story about plain old commerce.

As it happened, Cadbury had little need of the looser entry criteria, because it was able to cite some impressive commercial metrics. The awards entry, prepared by agency VCCP, was titled 'There's a glass & a half in everyone: How intrinsic purpose can transform a brand's fortunes'. It told the story of how a four-year campaign had helped rebuild the Cadbury brand and increased annual revenue by £261 million.

The campaign centred on the idea of generosity—a reference to the brand's Quaker roots and its long-standing product claim about containing a glass and a half of milk in every bar. TV ads told emotional tales of interpersonal generosity and gratitude. In one, a little girl ducks into a cornershop while her mother is stressed and distracted, then exchanges her favourite buttons and trinkets for a bar of Dairy Milk. The shop owner plays along and the girl rushes out to say happy birthday to her mother, who tears up in surprise. In another, an old man grudgingly returns balls that keep flying over the garden fence from the kids playing next door, until one day a bar of Dairy Milk flies over and two kids peek over to say 'You don't have to return that one, Mr Thompson'. In a third, a boy on a bus is holding a bar of Dairy Milk and his mum tells him to save it for later. Turning round, he notices a teenage girl crying and hesitantly offers some of his bar. She shakes her head, but is touched and grateful. The mother notices this and says "Go on then, just one" to the boy, who has learned a lesson about how generosity can feel good. In each case, the endline appears: "There's a glass and a half in everyone."

The awards entry case study video shows clips from these

tales, subtitled with commercial metrics. "Over five years, total Cadbury value sales rose 22%," says the text beneath the girl weeping on the bus. "It is estimated that due to advertising annual Cadbury sales were £261m higher at the end of the period than at the start," says the text beneath the boy sadly glancing at the girl. Notably, all the metrics relate to the commercial outcomes, with little mention of how this 'social purpose' winner made a difference on the social front.

When you dig into the details, you eventually find mention of a charity called Age UK, which does valuable work to combat loneliness among older people. It turns out Cadbury has donated some profits from the campaign towards this charity—all of which is laudable, but nothing revolutionary. As we've seen, companies have long donated to charities— it's one of the more useful things businesses do. What is new is the way purpose encourages companies to make themselves the centre of the story, while the charity (the socially purposeful organisation) is relegated to the small print. There was a time when it was considered graceless to donate to charity and be vocal about it. Now companies go much further, using the donation as the premise for constructing their entire, lucrative brand image.

According to Cadbury, it's deeper than a brand image. The senior marketing director behind the campaign is quoted as saying: "Aligning Cadbury behind a clear brand purpose— generous instinct—has been transformative for our brand. It's given the team a north star to guide our decisions."

Nine months after the first 'Happy Birthday Mum' ad was released in January 2018, British newspapers reported on another side to Cadbury. "Cadbury's US owners paid zero corporation tax in UK despite profits rocketing more than 700 per cent to £185 million" said the Daily Mail.[58] "This is outrageous," commented Labour Shadow Chancellor John McDonnell, adding: "This will do nothing but anger people who are going out to work every day, paying their taxes through PAYE." Alex Cobham, chief executive of the Tax Justice Network, said Mondelez was doing "a piece of financial engineering that is very sad given Cadbury's long history of working to generate value in the communities where they work." He added: "Mondelez [the parent company] are stripping value out, by siphoning off taxable profits from the UK through large intra-group dividend payments."

The story was the latest in a succession of similar reports stretching back to the hostile takeover of Cadbury by Kraft Foods in 2009. Questions were raised in Parliament in December 2015.[59] The Guardian reported that Cadbury paid no tax on profits of £96.5 million in 2014.[60] The Financial Times reported on "Cadbury: The great tax fudge" in 2013.[61] The investigation revealed how Cadbury's history of tax avoidance extended back more than a decade before the takeover, and was described by former senior executives as "highly aggressive".

Is it cynical to wonder where Cadbury's 'north star' was during the years of avoiding tax on hundreds of millions in profits? Or is it cynical not to? Paying tax might be the single most socially purposeful any business can do—it's an excellent way to fund schools, hospitals, public transport and services for the elderly. Maybe it's legally defensible to use clever accounting tricks to avoid it, but basing your next marketing campaign on generosity ought to get you chased from the room, not applauded onto the awards stage.

There are more dimensions to the story. In recent years, Cadbury has existed in an increasingly uncomfortable environment when it comes to HFSS (high in fat, salt and sugar) marketing regulations. New rules introduced in 2022 include a ban on the promotion of HFSS foods in key locations such as store entrances, aisle ends and checkouts. Health authorities consider this crucial given that 40% of Cadbury sales come from impulse purchases. A more recent Cadbury advert shows such a purchase taking place: a father at a petrol station points out a bar beside the till, then gifts it to his daughter who (it turns out) is the woman behind the till. It's unclear whether this would be covered by the regulations, and it seems churlish to ask given that the ad is depicting such an emotional bonding moment.

For these purposes, it's not necessary to take a position on whether HFSS regulations are an excessive intervention by the nanny state, or a valid response to an obesity problem that grew during lockdown, when comfort eating became a valuable source of revenue for Cadbury and others. Whatever your view, the larger point is that, as a democratic society, with cross-party support, the UK decided that it would be socially beneficial to sell fewer of these products—saving on costs to the National Health Service and generally improving people's quality of life. Nor are these the only social benefits. A 2023 report by Ethical Consumer rates Cadbury as "poor" and a "brand to avoid" for issues related to tax conduct, use of palm oil, deforestation and plastic and packaging—and particularly for revelations in a Channel 4 Dispatches documentary claiming that that 10-year-old children were using machetes to harvest cocoa destined for the Cadbury supply chain.[62]

None of this is to portray Cadbury as some uniquely malevolent actor in the world. I'm partial to a Dairy Milk, relaxed about the marketing of it, and as susceptible as anyone else to emotional tales of human relationships. But the disconnect should be clear. At the IPA Effectiveness Awards, the ad industry hails Cadbury not only as an example of a successful commercial campaign, but explicitly as the 'social purpose' campaign of the year. Everyone involved goes away feeling reassured about the socially positive contribution of the industry to society. Meanwhile, out there in society, people are specifically asking for less of this kind of advertising, wondering if it's OK for Cadbury to pay more tax in future, and making documentaries about brands to avoid.

It's notable that all this is happening through the IPA. Having introduced its new social purpose category, it handed the award to Cadbury on 10 October 2022, halfway through the ill-fated prime ministership of Liz Truss, who rode to power on a promise of tax cuts and deregulation. On behalf of its ad agency members, the IPA welcomed her appointment in a statement that ended: "Lastly, we hope that our new Prime Minister can swiftly deliver on her promises of cancelling the planned rise in corporation tax."[63] At the time, the Labour party and most economics commentators regarded the Truss policy as wildly irresponsible. But no one in adland appeared to mind the IPA openly lobbying on its behalf. Whatever your view on the tax burden, it's hard to see much moral consistency in a tax-lobbying industry body awarding a tax-avoiding business for a campaign about generosity, in order to lend the ad industry a socially purposeful glow.

None of this stopped the Cadbury campaign being widely hailed. Leading commentator Mark Ritson, for the most part a reliable sceptic on purpose, wrote as if he had finally seen the light: "In a true act of marketing generosity, Cadbury and its team of extraordinary marketers show others the way." Berating himself for previous negativity, he argues that it would be idiotic to dwell on the taxation issue, because: "Ultimately, most consumers do not understand what corporation tax is, let alone who isn't paying it. Telly, not taxes, drives brand perceptions and clever-clogs columnists should remember that market-oriented point."[64]

Purpose critics are often branded cynics, but nothing strikes me as more cynical than this view. In an article at the time, I described it as a kind of "purpose nihilism".[65] So what if there's hypocrisy, so what if there's no real social impact, so what if it's taking people for a ride. As long as the public like the ad, it's all good. If it works, it works.

On a commercial level, it makes sense. The point of an ad is to drive up sales, and there's every reason why Cadbury should win commercial effectiveness awards, or creativity and craft awards. But social purpose claims to be, and ought to be, a different category. Elsewhere, Mark Ritson writes more lucidly that "The purpose of purpose is purpose."[66] In other words, the goal of a social purpose campaign should be to drive social outcomes, and that's how it should be judged. Focusing on commercial metrics ought to be beside the point, or even cause for suspicion as it casts doubt on the motives behind the campaign. But the purpose movement forces everyone, including marketing commentators, into this tangled position where purpose and profit keep switching places as the north star, often mid-column or even mid-sentence.

For Ritson, there is another reason why the campaign is remarkable. He sees it as a lesson in the value of longevity, pointing to the long tenure of the marketing team: "At Mondelez, there is a team of exceptional women who run marketing for Cadbury. And it's not just that they are all seasoned, outstanding marketing people. It's that they have been working on the brand for many years."[67] By this reading, it's a source of celebration that the generosity campaign comes from the same people who rode out the tax-avoiding years that were continuing as the campaign launched. Writing at a time when the UK was on its fourth Chancellor in four months, Ritson argued for the value of long tenure if you want to get anything done. Any chancellor might argue for the value of corporation tax in helping them do it.

I tell this story at length because it's indicative of how purpose acts as a distraction from any sober consideration of actual social purpose, which exists primarily in the not-for-profit and public sectors. This is not to set up a simple binary of 'corporate = bad' and 'public/non-profit = good'. There are plenty of social benefits to businesses doing what businesses do, just as there are plenty of structural flaws and wasted resources in the public sector. But there is a higher logic in recognising the distinctness of these spheres in society, even as they continually interact and play off each other. The past decade has seen a bloated corporate sphere encroaching on areas far beyond itself, often posing as the solution to problems that business itself has caused.

We've seen how this pattern plays out at multiple levels. In the employment market, charities and non-profits compete with the private sector for idealistic young graduates. In creative industry awards, charities find the social purpose limelight stolen by washing powders and deodorants. In the public realm, cynicism builds around social causes as each becomes associated with another brand planting its flag. Think Pride, think Skittles. Think maternal mental health, think Maltesers. Think food waste, think Hellmann's. Think toxic masculinity, think Gillette.

The corporate takeover comes full circle as purposeful brands begin earnestly lecturing charities on how to do better. "Businesses like Virgin and Innocent lead the way in expressing their sense of purpose; charities can learn by their example," says leadership coach Carla Miller in the Guardian.[68] "For charities to operate successfully in the new purpose-led landscape, it will involve a change in mindset with a focus on sharing long-term goals alongside corporate partners... Share the vision with the business world—or even better create it with them," urges executive coach Kate Adams in Fast Company.[69] "As we've entered the era of brand purpose, businesses, not charities, are seen as being the best placed to deliver social value. Our blog looks at what charity brands can do in response to reclaim trust and social purpose," says Dan DuFour, brand strategist at ad agency The Team.[70]

It's not hard to imagine how these messages must land in a sector that knows its 'reason for being' pretty clearly, and decided at the outset that it wasn't for profit. On the plus side, charities retain one advantage over their new competitors: exemption from corporation tax. Alas, during the purpose years, it hasn't been a major point of difference.

Purpose is parasitical on creativity

'There's a glass and a half in everyone' is a variation on the 'glass and a half' campaign that Cadbury first introduced in 1928: a product claim that promised a glass and a half of full fat milk in every 200g bar of chocolate. The addition of 'in everyone' is a way to tweak it into a purposeful message—something that has become a common flex in the age of purpose.

'Beanz Meanz Heinz' is considered one of the classic slogans—composed by adman Maurice Drake during a session in London pub, The Victoria. It was a way to ward off cheaper supermarket competition by making Heinz the definitive name in its category: all captured in a little three-word poem. In 2021, the purpose flex was again deployed, turning the line into 'Beanz Meanz More': part of a drive to emphasise the health benefits of beans and 'evolve conversations' around the brand.[71]

'Gillette: The Best a Man Can Get' is another enduring slogan, launched in 1989 to associate Gillette with product excellence in its category. (Incidentally, the brand was already 88 years old at this point, having been founded by the excellently named King C. Gillette, a Utopian socialist who believed that all industry should be taken over by a single corporation owned by the public, and that everyone in the USA should live in a single city called Metropolis, powered by Niagara Falls. Elon Muskian eccentricity has a long history.) In 2019, Gillette celebrated the 30-year anniversary of 'The Best a Man Can Get' by deploying its own version of the purpose flex. New slogan: 'The Best Men Can Be'.

What was lost in rhythm and rhyme was gained in purposeful resonance. The campaign launched with a film that earnestly questioned Gillette's previous slogan. Against a backdrop of #metoo headlines, the script began: "Is this the best a man can get? Is it? We can't hide from it. It's been going on far too long. We can't laugh it off." After further musings about toxic masculinity, intercut with scenes of fathers breaking up fights and voicing empowering affirmations to their daughters, the script finished: "It's only by challenging ourselves to do more that we can get closer to our best. We are taking action at thebestmencanbe.org"

Praised in some liberal circles, the ad became one of the most disliked videos on YouTube, sparking calls for a boycott amid the kind of culture war furore that would later be repeated with Bud Light. "Gillette brand takes a hit as '#metoo' ad backfires" reported Marketing Week in the aftermath. Six months later, Reuters reported strong sales across all P&G products barring Gillette, on which it took an $8bn write-down. This was ascribed to changes in men's grooming habits and a declining razor market, but most believe the ad controversy didn't help.

There's a glass and a half in everyone, Beanz Meanz More, The Best Men Can Be… add in the switch from I Heart NYC to We Heart NYC and you see a pattern of purpose co-opting the slogans of the past to project new messages for the present. It can be read as a metaphor for the way purpose works in general. Whether it's Hellmann's pondering its purpose after 110 years of history, or Gillette mounting its soapbox after 118 years of selling razors, there's a familiar pattern whereby purpose stands on the shoulders of giants in order to raise its placard. A truth obscured by the Start With Why mantra is that all these marketers are only in a position to ponder their 'why' because of decades of commercial, product-focused, hard-working advertising that gave them the budget to hire the purpose agency and book the Super Bowl slots.

The purpose flex is echoed at the institutional level. Within the ad industry, rather than creating its own awards and institutions, purpose has taken over the existing ones. At a particular high watermark in 2022, purposeful campaigns accounted for 17 of the 21 winners in the so-called creativity and craft categories at Cannes, and 48 of the 78 winners at D&AD.[72] It would be straightforward to have parallel purpose categories that judge social purpose on its merits, but the point is that the competing agencies aren't interested in winning those. If the award is billed as 'creative', it enables them to describe themselves afterwards as an outstanding creative agency, which is useful for attracting clients ranging from airlines to banks to oil companies. If the awards were more honestly described as purpose awards, or 'creativity for good' awards, many potential clients might see the agency as a niche 'for good' agency and not quite the right fit. What agencies desire is the cachet and prestige associated with historic creative awards: prestige that they can cash out in commercial accounts and lucrative career moves.

Meanwhile, at the University of the Arts London (UAL), the next generation of creative professionals receives training in design, film, fashion, advertising and more— except now they do it under the watchful eye of a new Chief Social Purpose Officer, whose role is to channel this creativity towards a purposeful agenda and prepare students for the brave new corporate world. The position is currently occupied by Polly Mackenzie, former Head of Strategy for the 2010 Liberal Democrat election campaign and Director of Policy from 2010 to 2015. The new generation of politically aware students appears unaware of the role she played in the tuition fees u-turn that had their fellow students incandescent with rage as recently as 2011.

The appointment may have something to do with her boss, President and Vice-Chancellor James Purnell, former Work and Pensions Secretary and Culture Secretary in Gordon Brown's government, before resigning with an overt swipe against his leader, and eventually leaving Labour Party politics altogether. A year into his tenure at UAL, he posted the following progress report:

> "A year on, we've found that social purpose is fertile ground. Our strategy, which we will publish next week, is built around it. What have we learned from this process? First, that we are joining a global movement. From Simon Sinek's

TED lecture to the 80,000 hours movement, for good or ill, there's a buzz around the concept."[73]

There he is again: Simon Sinek hovering behind this new movement that is now influencing a former cabinet minister and Vice Chancellor at a leading creative university. It's a remarkable achievement for a thesis built on debunked brain science and retrofitted case studies.

Why is all this bad for society? Because creative excellence is something that should be allowed to grow and flourish, without the cuckoo of purpose squatting in its nest. To strike a parochial note, the UK has a strong story to tell in the field of commercial creativity, with creative industries contributing £115.9 billion to the economy in 2019, and growing at a rate that exceeds the national average by a factor of five.[74] Econometrics to one side, you don't have to be a hopeless romantic to believe that creativity might also have intrinsic value in its own right: it's one of the better things that humans do. Both economically and spiritually, it might be nice to live in a society where creativity is celebrated on its own terms, not because it is serving the higher master of purpose. Purpose is a deadening force that conscripts creativity towards political ends. That way, a lot of bad art lies.

Purpose distracts from climate action

In January 2018, BlackRock CEO Larry Fink published *A Sense of Purpose*, the first in a series of annual letters to the world's CEOs that spelt out the purpose agenda and urged every company to follow it. Around the same time, BlackRock welcomed a new Chief Investment Officer for Sustainable Investing, who would lead efforts to incorporate so-called 'ESG' activities across the firm's investment activities.

Originating in the UN's 'Who Cares Wins' report of 2004, ESG stood for Environmental, Social and Governance: the three measures by which purposeful corporations would be judged. The precise meaning of each term, and how it should be measured, remains inconsistent. 'Environmental' broadly stands for sustainability and climate action. 'Social' stands for diversity and representation. 'Governance' stands for corporate accountability, but in the 'stakeholder' sense where a company is answerable to everybody in vaguely defined ways. Over time, ESG has become broadly synonymous with the 'do well by doing good' ethos of the purpose movement.

BlackRock's new appointee was Tariq Fancy, a one-time investment banker who had left to start up an educational non-profit called Rumie. But when the BlackRock offer came, he saw it as an unmissable opportunity to do good at scale. As he later explained: "BlackRock was then and remains today the world's largest investment firm. At the end of June [2021], it had \$9.5 trillion under management and was closing in on what the Wall Street Journal called the 'once unthinkable': $10 trillion in assets.[75] Managed well, that kind of firepower could create far more positive impact for the world than possible running Rumie."

Over the next 21 months, Tariq Fancy enjoyed a unique vantage point from which to see the inner workings of the ESG movement in which he sincerely believed. By September 2019, disillusioned and alarmed, he left BlackRock and began work on a three-part essay about his experience. The Secret Diary of a Sustainable Investor shed light on what Tariq Fancy saw as a doomed attempt to answer "inconvenient truths with convenient fantasies". Towards the end, he writes: "In sounding the alarm, my hope is to expose this illusion for what it is: a dangerous fantasy that primarily serves the interests of the oldest and the richest, and all at the expense of the youngest, the poorest, and the most diverse and historically underserved communities in the world today."

The story had started with high hopes: "I sincerely believed that while sustainable investing was not perfect, it was a step in the right direction in the critical question of how business and society should intersect in the 21st century." But the sense of unease began to rise as Fancy attended an ESG awards dinner in Stockholm: "I grew up believing that the warm feeling of saving the world generally only came through some level of selflessness and sacrifice, almost as a necessary cost, in line with the images of those supreme beings who had joined the Peace Corps and were in some faraway land working happily in the service of others. Yet it seemed that much of that same excitement and satisfying feeling of purpose was here too, in a chic venue with champagne and chocolate, and without quite as much sacrifice thanks to innovative new models of business, technology and finance."

Halfway through his time at BlackRock, Covid strikes and Tariq Fancy notes a dissonance in the corporate response. All around him, companies are clamouring for the government to take systemic action to tackle this shorter-term emergency. Yet, faced with the longer-term risk of climate change, the belief is that voluntary action will solve the problem. "Rather than relying on voluntary compliance to flatten the Covid-19 curve, our government actively ensured that lockdown measures were mandatory through forced closures and penalties. Those who didn't adhere to the rules endangered us all, so we were generally fine with stiff penalties that applied to anyone caught flouting the guidelines." Fancy quotes William Nordhaus, a Nobel Prize-winning economist, calling for a similar response to the climate challenge: "Economics points to one inconvenient truth about climate change policy. And that is that in order to be effective, the policies have to raise the price of carbon, or CO_2, and in doing that correct the externality of the marketplace."

The point is driven home with a basketball analogy: "If you want to change the behavior of all of the players in the game, you have to change the rules of the game for everyone… Instead, on sustainability issues, we're currently being told that our hope lies in standing back and relying on some players sometimes deciding to pursue good sportsmanship, purely voluntarily, even if playing dirty helps them fulfill their legal duty to score maximum points." Tariq Fancy quotes an anonymous portfolio manager at BlackRock making precisely this point: "I believe in climate change. If we had a price on carbon, I'd lower my carbon footprint overnight—and so would everyone else. But it makes no sense to do it alone and put myself at a disadvantage, and it's not what I'm legally supposed to do or paid to do."

Fine, but isn't it still useful for companies to do *something*, rather than just wait for government intervention? Tariq Fancy initially wants to believe that, but reluctantly concludes the situation is worse. It's not just that ESG is an imperfect solution; it's that it's actively making the real solutions harder to implement. He commissions research showing how the public is influenced by pro-ESG headlines, leading to a feedback loop where companies point to that support as further justification for what they do. He cites another research paper showing that "quick fix" solutions to address the climate crisis have a "pernicious effect" in that they "decrease support for substantive policies by providing false hope that problems can be tackled without imposing considerable costs".[76] As Fancy notes: "This set of observations led me to wonder: what if the work I had been doing at BlackRock was actively harming society, by misleading the public and delaying overdue government reforms?"

Despite this dawning reality, Fancy sees his boss Larry Fink making increasingly influential interventions, including a January 2021 interview with Bloomberg where he asserts: "I prefer capitalists self-regulate."[77] In Fancy's view, this effectively puts Fink to the right of Milton Friedman, who is widely quoted for his view that businesses should focus solely on profits, but less widely quoted for his view that civil servants "elected through a political process" should look out for the public interest. Going back to the basketball analogy: "A market economy is at its core a collection of rules. No rules, no market." If you believe in markets, you have to believe in some degree of government intervention, just as love of basketball requires the existence of referees.

Tariq Fancy makes more granular arguments about the misperceptions around what 'divestment' means (usually a way to manage exposure and brand image rather than change the underlying reality), the false incentive structures of ESG (he notes that ESG products generally carry higher fees than non-ESG products, making them a useful revenue stream), and the hopeless mishmash of ESG scores (which allow a company like FTX to enjoy a higher rating than Exxon Mobil on the eve of FTX's collapse). But overall, Fancy returns to the point that ESG represents the market itself trying to fix one of the biggest market failures in history: "In my role at BlackRock, I was helping to popularize an idea that the answer to a sustainable future runs through ESG and sustainability and green products, or in other words, that the answer to the market's failure to serve the long-term public interest is, of course, more market." The only thing that stops a bad guy with a gun is a good guy with a gun, goes the NRA argument derided by the liberal mainstream. But the same liberal mainstream is beguiled by the do-well-by-doing-good guys who police the corporate world.

It's worth telling this story at length because it was a powerful and rare intervention in the purpose debate. The Economist called it "riveting" and the Financial Times later reflected: "With hindsight, Fancy looks less like a heretic and more like ESG's Cassandra."[78]

Tariq Fancy's personal journey also maps onto the wider debate. Much of the ESG movement was built on the evidence base of a single influential paper, published in 2016 by Mozaffar Khan, George Serafeim and Aaron Yoon. In a paper titled Corporate Sustainability: First Evidence on Materiality, the authors concluded that stocks rating highly on corporate sustainability measures delivered reliably higher returns, amounting to 3 to 6% per year, or roughly 50% more than average market returns over 21 years.[79] Despite being described by its authors as representing only 'first evidence', the paper's conclusions were eagerly embraced by a growing complex of ESG fund managers and unregulated ESG ratings bodies.

As is often the case, the debunking takes a while to catch up, gains less attention than the original claims, and is then slowly proven right by the gradual and inexorable unfolding of reality. In a 2022 paper titled Corporate Sustainability: A Model Uncertainty Analysis of Materiality, Luca Berchicci and Andrew King pointed out the implausibility of a sustained 3-6% investment advantage hiding in plain sight in commercially available data for all these years, which goes against all theories of informational market efficiency.[80] Further pushback came in the form of a 2021 paper by Sony Kapoor and Felix Goltz, entertainingly titled Honey, I Shrunk the ESG Alpha. The paper digs deep into the original data and finds that any growth is likely accounted for by conventional 'quality' factors that are wrapped up in the hazy G ('governance') of ESG. Once you correct for that, there is no relevant improvement related to sustainability.[81]

None of these debunking authors is a climate-denying

outlier—exactly the opposite. Andrew King, Professor at Questrom School of Business, Boston University, is a carbon tax advocate who worries that, "ESG investing is like a comforting fairytale that allows you to drift off to sleep. Why worry when you are being told that your 401(k) can beat the market while solving for climate change?"[82] Sony Kapoor is a Professor of Climate, Geoeconomics, and Finance, and managing director of the Nordic Institute for Finance, Technology, Sustainability, and Society. He concludes that, "Most ESG investing is a ruse to launder reputations, maximise fees and assuage guilt."[83]

But against this backdrop of serious critique, the response from the business world has been muted. Larry Fink declined invitations to debate or respond to his former colleague Tariq Fancy, though there has been a notable pulling back from purpose in his 2023 CEO letter. Meanwhile, in the marketing world, most people are barely aware this debate is even taking place, despite ad agencies being among the early super spreaders of the purpose meme, and despite the machinations of ESG lying behind almost every brief that lands in agency in-trays.

The issues nevertheless bubble to the surface in various controversies and mishaps. Bulb is hailed as a best-in-class example of energy marketing for a new generation—listed as a B Corp by the new, voguish self-regulation body—but then spectacularly goes under with taxpayers once again riding to the rescue.[84] Innocent is hailed as a poster child for sustainable marketing, but then has an ad banned by the Advertising Standards Authority for overclaiming about "fixing up the planet".[85] The awards event at Cannes is interrupted by a previous winner ostentatiously invading the stage to return his awards for airline and automotive advertising, which he now regrets—the kind of worthy but grandiose act that the ad world regards as heroism.

Meanwhile, the most systemic response from adland involves a story worth sharing.

On 21 November 2023, Channel 4 aired an ad titled 'The Good Advert', timed to coincide with climate change documentary 'The Great Climate Fight'.

The 30-second spot opens with an apparent technical glitch, before a hesitant voice (comedian Simon Amstell) comes in and apologises for being an advert. The script:

> Hello... I'm... I'm an advert and... I can't, I can't... I just feel awful about it. It's erm... I'm always asking you to spend more. The message needs to be... You need to go out and spend more time in nature! With people you love, perhaps. Because haven't we all got a part to play?

The endline appears: The future is ours to create.

The ad turned out to be the brainchild of Purpose Disruptors, an organisation describing itself as "a network of advertising insiders working together to reshape our industry to tackle climate change". The ad was scripted and filmed by regular collaborators Iris Worldwide.

Earlier on the same day, the Guardian had published an extended critique of consumerism, titled 'The Guardian view on festive marketing: stop spending like there's no tomorrow'.[86] This came in the wake of the Guardian's positive coverage of UK Christmas ads, which are the equivalent of the Super Bowl in the US when it comes to eager press attention. The editorial nevertheless bemoaned excessive consumption and cited specific evidence for the carbon impact of advertising:

> "Clearly advertising shifts units, but at what cost? The Guardian reports that an award-winning 2018 campaign for Audi saw the marque gain 132,700 in extra car sales, which produced the equivalent annual greenhouse gas emissions of Uganda. Promoting a lifestyle of overconsumption – SUVs rather than hatchbacks, long-haul flights not rail travel – is good for business but bad for the planet."

As it happens, this evidence comes from the same people behind the Simon Amstell ad: a combination of Purpose Disruptors and Iris Worldwide.[87] Although it's quoted with confidence by the Guardian, the research has since been discredited—and it doesn't take much insight to see why.[88] Is it credible that a single ad campaign for Audi would produce the annual greenhouse gas emissions of Uganda? If that was close to true, and you multiply it by all the car ad campaigns that ran that year and every other year, wouldn't the planet already be a charred cinder by now?

It turns out the researchers used the simple methodology of taking the claimed increase in Audi sales (132,700) and multiplying it by the lifetime emissions of a single Audi car. Known as Advertised Emissions, this method ignores how most of those sales were going to happen anyway, because the effect of car advertising (even more so than most categories) is mainly about competition between which brands get bought. No one who is not already in need of a car goes out and buys an Audi because the ad convinced them. If the ad is successful, some might decide to buy an Audi instead of a BMW. Even ignoring that factor, to put Audi sales down to their most recent ad campaign shows a touching faith in the short-term effects of advertising: the reality is that brands are built over decades, not months. Most sales today are down to advertising that a brand did ten years ago. This doesn't stop agencies making inflated claims of commercial effectiveness in their case studies, but it doesn't mean they should be mirrored when it comes to the consequential issue of climate.

All this leads to real-world effects. The people behind Advertised Emissions proudly state that the methodology has been embraced by influential industry players. You might wonder how this is skewing thinking around climate. After all, a reader might understandably think 'If only we could stop this one Audi campaign, we'd be making a huge dent in global carbon emissions'. An Audi marketing manager might choose to scale back their activity and claim a Uganda-sized positive result in their annual sustainability report. None of it connects to reality, barely affecting an ounce of carbon in the air, and creating a false idea of meaningful action in the process.

The story gets stranger. The Guardian editorial links to another article, published on the same day, which repeats the Audi/Uganda claim and goes further:

"Similar trends are evident in the air travel industry. More than half of Delta Air Lines' approximately $151m ad spend from October 2022 to October 2023, for example, was spent advertising long-haul flights, encouraging travellers to rack up air miles to use for more travel, and pushing upgrades to premium classes, although the airline also spent tens of millions of dollars to advertise its commitment to 'sustainable aviation fuels'".[89]

Who is Delta Air Lines' ad agency, specifically for long haul flights? It turns out to be Iris Worldwide, the agency behind The Good Advert. Their website also showcases work for Bentley's luxury SUVs, Jeep, Mini, VW, Volvo and Lamborghini.

Hypocrisy is the tribute vice pays to virtue, said François de La Rochefoucauld. It's always easy to call out examples and it shouldn't necessarily dissuade imperfect actors from doing good things. But the deeper point is that The Good Advert isn't doing much good for anyone. On one level, it's an ad agency taking a cheap shot at its own industry, while happily playing for the other team the rest of the year. The Simon Amstell script might at least have been more interesting if it had acknowledged some of the complexities: "Then again, I did help fund this climate change programme you're watching, so it's complicated isn't it?" As we've seen earlier, advertising can deliver basic social benefits by doing its job well.

On another level, Iris Worldwide and Purpose Disruptors are feeding a narrative that climate action must always be associated with guilt, deprivation and not having nice things—which is usually delivered in a tone of condescending elitism. 'You need to go out and spend more time in nature,' says the script from the ad agency, to which a viewer might reasonably respond: 'And what are you doing exactly? I've just sat down after another day as a nurse / teacher / construction worker / delivery driver / job seeker. I've just got the kids to bed, bought them a few Christmas presents online, done the supermarket shop without which we'd starve. Now you want me to go out into nature? It's 9pm. Shall I see you in the local woods? Can I buy a torch off Amazon Prime first?'

Even for an audience watching a climate change documentary, it's an expensive missed opportunity. Climate change advertising could be aspirational: cleaner air, nicer cities, better cars, cheaper energy bills. Ad agencies could have made solar panels and water butts cool by now. Ad agencies with a 30-second slot in peak time could use it to say something useful: support this charity, donate to this cause, buy this green product. Instead, it's promoting a self-referential hashtag that garnered almost zero interaction on social media.

It's a sign of the dysfunction around the climate debate and the way purpose only obfuscates the real issues. François de la Rochefoucauld also said "We are so accustomed to disguise ourselves to others, that in the end, we become disguised to ourselves." Remove the haze of purpose from the climate debate, and we might start to see ourselves, and reality, more clearly.

Purpose is the trader in the temple

If you're reading this in the order in which I wrote it, you'll hopefully remember me referencing the story of Jesus in the temple, driving out the traders whose best-selling product line consisted of doves to be used in ritual sacrifices. It would be remiss to end this critique without addressing the main poster child for the purposeful traders of our age: Dove.

You might live in that fabled land outside the marketing industry, in which case maybe you loosely associate Dove with roll-on deodorants, bars of moisturising soap, and ads that use the colour white a lot. But within adland, Dove enjoys an elevated status as one of the trailblazers of the purpose movement. Having been a solid part of Unilever's portfolio since 1957, the brand sought to broaden from soap to the wider beauty category by launching the Campaign for Real Beauty in 2004, consisting of both the Real Beauty Pledge and the parallel Self-Esteem Project. Since then, it has associated itself with a social mission to "make beauty a source of confidence, not anxiety".

One of the instigators was chief creative officer Joah Santos, who applied a method he described as POV: Purpose, Objective, Vision. From the beginning, Dove was astute enough to add a gloss of science to its social mission, commissioning a white paper with named contributors including Dr. Nancy Etcoff of Harvard University, Dr. Susie Orbach of London School of Economics, and Dr. Jennifer Scott and Heidi D'Agostino, from StrategyOne, a subsidiary of Edelman Public Relations.[90]

Although the white paper has the air of social science,

it is primarily a market research exercise conducted by StrategyOne, designed to prove the existence of the societal problem that Dove would build its brand around solving. The report opens with a quote from Keats: "'Beauty is truth, truth beauty'—that is all ye know on earth, and all ye need to know." Cultural historians will note that the word 'truth' was going through an interesting evolution around this time. Over the next two years, both the American Dialect Society and Merriam-Webster would make 'truthiness' their word of the year: the quality of seeming or being felt to be true, based on emotions rather than evidence.

The white paper involved a survey of 3,200 women aged 18-64. The headline was that only 2% considered themselves 'beautiful' (revised to 4% in a follow-up 2011 study). This provided the shocking figure that justified Dove's campaign to bolster women's self-esteem. Less reported was the finding that 72% of women said they rated their beauty as average, and only 13% saw themselves as less beautiful or physically attractive than others. It's also worth noting that an obvious response bias creeps into the framing of questions like these. Is any of it really a finding about the participants' inherent insecurity, or more a wish not to appear vain when being asked about their appearance?

The research would later be dramatised in a #ChooseBeautiful campaign, in which adjacent entrances in public spaces were labelled 'Beautiful' and 'Average'. The resulting brand film framed the exercise as a pop science experiment, in which under-confident women chose mainly to go through the 'Average' entrance, barring a few who chose 'Beautiful' because they were sufficiently empowered, or because their mother was with them and insisted they walk through it—all to a background of swelling piano music. Again, the fact that this is a forced choice taking place in a highly public space might make it evidence of socially acceptable modesty rather than inner self-loathing. Kat Gordon, founder of the 3% Conference, which advocates more female leadership in advertising, called the campaign "heavy-handed and manipulative".[91] Arwa Mahdawi wrote in the Guardian that Dove "has mastered the art of passing off somewhat passive-aggressive and patronising advertising as super-empowering, ultra PR-able social commentary".[92]

In this case, at least women were making their own self-assessment. Dove's Real Beauty campaign had begun with billboard portraits of what were described as regular women rather than professional models. The campaign included an interactive Times Square billboard that invited passers-by to vote on whether a particular model was 'Fat or Fab' or 'Wrinkled or Wonderful', with the results dynamically updated and displayed on the billboard. It's reported that 'fat' overtook the 'fab' number—an early example of the dangers of crowdsourced marketing.[93]

This public rating of physical appearance didn't seem likely to boost self-esteem, and soon Dove learned to be more subtle. 'Tested on Real Curves' was a poster campaign featuring a range of 'real' women unlike the usual models seen in ad campaigns. It was nevertheless a curated sample. Writing in The Atlantic in 2007, Virginia Postrel noted that, "The 'real women' pictured in the thigh-cream billboards may not have looked like supermodels, but they were all young, with symmetrical faces, feminine features, great skin, white teeth, and hourglass shapes. Even the most zaftig had relatively flat stomachs and clearly defined waists. These pretty women were not a random sample of the population. Dove diversified the portrait of beauty without abandoning the concept altogether."[94]

There was a lively row when photo retoucher Pascal Dangin told the New Yorker that he had made extensive edits to the campaign photos: "Do you know how much retouching was on that? But it was great to do, a challenge, to keep everyone's skin and faces showing the mileage but not looking unattractive." After that inadvertent moment of candour, he later appeared to row back the claims.[95]

The campaign received criticism for the way its stance conflicted with other brands in the Unilever stable. While Dove talked about women's self-esteem, Axe (also known as Lynx) continued to run campaigns based on stereotypically sexualised women, while other products included SlimFast diet bars and Fair & Lovely, a controversial skin-lightening product marketed primarily in India—now rebranded as Glow & Lovely with previous references to 'whitening' removed from the language.

The high point in Dove's campaign came with Real Beauty Sketches in 2013. Based on Joah Santos's strategy and credited to Portuguese copywriter Hugo Veiga, the film would become one of the most viral of the decade, setting the template for similar ads to follow. The choreography is always similar, with nervous participants walking into a cavernous space to take part in a social experiment orchestrated by the wise and all-seeing brand. In this case, the room contained Gil Zamora, a male forensic artist from the San Jose Police Department. Placed behind a screen, the women were asked to describe their facial appearance to the artist. They reply in mainly self-effacing terms. "Tell me about your chin,'" says the man. "It kind of protrudes a little bit," says the woman. "Your jaw?" says the man. "My mom told me I had a big jaw," says the woman. We hear this over soft piano music—these ads would always land differently without it.

Afterwards, another stranger, who has met the participants only briefly, walks in and gives an alternative description of them to the sketch artist, this time in more flattering terms. "Her chin? It was a nice, thin chin," says the stranger. "Cute nose," says another stranger. "She had nice eyes, they lit up when she spoke," says another stranger.

As the piano music swells, the original women are led back in and shown one sketch based on their own description (somewhat dour and plain-looking), then another based on the stranger's description (comparatively brighter and more flattering). Learning their lesson, the women tear up and realise how much they've been talking themselves down. "Do you think you're more beautiful than you say?" asks the male artist. "Yeah... Yes." says the woman hesitantly, continuing: "I should be more grateful." Another participant is shown hugging her boyfriend, having realised how unnecessarily insecure she was. "You are more beautiful than you think," says the endline as the Dove logo appears.

The film was a social media hit, expertly framed to generate an emotional response. But some commentators were concerned. "These ads still uphold the notion that, when it comes to evaluating ourselves and other women, beauty is paramount," wrote Ann Friedman in The Cut. "The goal shouldn't be to get women to focus on how we are all gorgeous in our own way. It should be to get women to do for ourselves what we wish the broader culture would do: judge each other based on intelligence and wit and ethical sensibility, not just our faces and bodies."[96] The criticism chimes with another underreported finding in the original Dove research, which was that "beauty and physical appearance are not the primary drivers of women's well-being"—coming behind factors such as family, friends, health, religious faith and professional success.

All this delivered undoubted commercial benefits for the brand. Ranked top in Ad Age's list of Campaigns of the Century, the work has been credited with raising sales from $2.5 billion to $4 billion over ten years.[97] Marketing commentator Mark Ritson has pointed out how the purposeful ads ran in parallel with many far more traditional product-centric ads—what the Dove team called their 'dual communications model'—so it's hard to separate out the impact of the two.[98] Nevertheless, the purposeful ads have to be credited with raising the salience of the brand, despite (or perhaps because of) the attendant controversies.

The question for this chapter, and for anyone interested in social impact beyond commercial sales, is whether this has delivered anything good for society. As always, that's harder to measure. One advantage of a societal mission is that it's hard to attribute blame to a soap brand if trends go in the wrong direction (which can be framed as all the more reason to fight the good fight), but easier to claim a share of credit if things improve.

The evidence from the last two decades has not been encouraging. Figures presented in a District of Columbia filing against Meta and Instagram show an alarming rise in suicide rates among 12-14 year old girls, self-poisoning among 13-15 year old girls, major depressive episodes in 14-15 year old girls, and depressive symptoms among eighth-grade girls over the course of 2001 to 2018. There is a particular spike around 2004, then a dramatic rise from 2011 onwards, which the filing describes as attributable to the rise of mobile phones and social media.

None of this bodes well for the success of the Self-Esteem Project, but Dove's more recent work has turned this into fertile ground. On TikTok, a #TurnYourBack campaign rails against beautifying filters on the platform. It's a worthy target, but the campaign takes the familiar purpose approach of funding the platform it criticises. A 'principle isn't a principle until it costs you something' approach might involve brands withdrawing from a platform that policy makers have discussed banning in the west. But commercial incentives mean the 'do well by doing good' approach is always more appealing: keep advertising to a key demographic, but frame it as resistance.

Social media spend has risen accordingly. At the start of 2023, marketing insight organisation WARC upgraded its ad spend forecast for TikTok by almost $2bn to $15.2bn, noting that 75% of marketers planned to increase their activity on the platform: a 52% increase in ad revenue over the previous year.[99] If social media platforms are largely to blame for the mental health crisis, it may be due to the ad-funded model that incentivises clickbait, confrontation and controversy.

Without the ads, there would be fewer problems for Dove to solve, or for other brands to 'lead the conversation' about.

Psychologists might ask other questions about the Dove approach. There's a well-known joke about how to make someone feel insecure: just go up to them and say "Look, whatever anyone else is saying, I think you're amazing." While it's framed as an empowering compliment, most people's natural reaction will be: "Wait, what is everyone else saying?"

You could say this has been Dove's brand strategy for 20 years. As I wrote in my first article about purpose in 2017, "Advertisers reinforce the insecurities they claim to fight, and introduce new insecurities that people didn't know they were supposed to have."[100]

Writer and comedian Mindy Kaling has written about the wave of 'empowerment' advertising aimed at women, with Dove at the forefront.

> "We just assume boys will be confident, like how your parents assume you will brush your teeth every morning without checking in on you in the bathroom. With girls, that assumption flies out the window. Suddenly, your parents are standing in the bathroom with you, watching you brush your teeth with encouraging, worried expressions on their faces. Sweetheart, you can do it! We know it's hard to brush your teeth! We love you! Which must make girls think, Yikes. Is brushing your teeth a really hard and scary thing to do? I thought it was just putting toothpaste on a toothbrush. I

get worried that telling girls how difficult it is to be confident implies a tacit expectation that girls won't be able to do it.

"The good news is that, as a country, we are all about telling girls to be confident. It's our new national pastime. Every day I see Twitter posts, Instagram campaigns, and hashtags that say things like 'We Will!' or 'Girls Can!' or 'Me Must, I Too!' on them. I think widespread, online displays of female self-confidence are good for people, especially men, to see. I just sometimes get the sneaking suspicion that corporations are co-opting 'girl confidence' language to rally girls into buying body wash. Be careful."[101]

'Be careful' continues to be good advice. In another Dove brand film, called Toxic Influence, mothers and daughters are led into the familiar cavernous space to talk to the all-powerful voice of Dove. Speaking from somewhere off-camera, the voice asks the mothers and daughters to discuss the effects of phone use and social media, to which the mothers give superficially complacent 'It's fine' answers. Dove then shows the participants a film in which deepfake technology has been used (apparently without permission) to put toxic beauty advice into the mouths of the mothers, who eagerly advise their daughters to use Botox, try powdered diet foods (maybe SlimFast) and file their teeth with a nail file. "That is not me!" cries one shocked mother.

"You wouldn't say that to your daughter," admonishes the

brand. "But she still hears it online, every day." The mothers are tearful. "A girl's greatest influence will always be her parents," reads the message on the big screen. "Always be talking" is the lesson they learn.

One day it would be interesting to run another kind of pop science experiment. Nervous Dove marketers could be led into a cavernous space and placed in front of a giant screen. The screen could show the mothers from the Toxic Influence ad saying 'Wait, so who funds these platforms?'. The piano could come in as a headline shows Unilever boosting its 2023 marketing spend by €500 million and opening 29 new digital marketing, media and ecommerce hubs.[102] The strings could swell as a caption appears: "Today, women are three times more likely than men to experience common mental health problems. In 1993, they were twice as likely."[103] A marketer could shed a tear as the Dove logo fades from a Covid nurse's face and an NHS logo appears in its place. A marketer's boyfriend could give her a hug as Radhika Parameswaran, professor of gender and media studies at Indiana University Bloomington, relates how Fair & Lovely holds a 70% share of India's skin-lightening market and "Just removing the word 'fair' is not enough."[104] Another marketer might murmur "I should be more grateful" as he reads about Unilever's profit margins on the back of price rises during the cost of living crisis.[105] The music could reach a crescendo as a group of Ukrainian amputees emerges from behind the screen and explains how Unilever doubled profits to 9.2 billion roubles and increased ad spend by 10% to 21.7 billion roubles after the Russian invasion.[106] Then the endline could appear: "But $2.5 billion to $4 billion in sales, so it's all good."

Harsh, maybe. But these are the conversations that purpose invites. Dove deserves praise for running a successful commercial campaign and smartly riding the cultural waves of the past two decades. But the purpose of purpose is purpose, and the impact of a social intervention has to be measured by its social outcomes. In that context, it's not enough to talk about starting conversations or generating social media impressions. When it comes to social impact, the warm feeling you get at the end of a Dove film is an unreliable guide. Truthiness isn't the same as truth.

Women's self-esteem is an important issue. The portrayal of girls and women in the media is an important issue. The growing mental health crisis is an important issue. All are too important to be used as springboards for soap marketing campaigns. Effective marketing is a good thing in its place. But when it comes via interventions in important social issues, it's stepping into another realm: call it the temple courtyard rather than the market square. Sooner or later, that will test the patience of a saint.

5.
What's the alternative?

The attempt to make heaven on earth
invariably produces hell.

– Karl Popper, *The Open Society and Its Enemies,* 1945

"Dear Americans, this July 4th dream of insurrection against corporate rule," read the first tweet to use the #occupywallstreet hashtag.

The tweet was posted on 4 July 2011 by a 'culture jamming' organisation and publication known as Adbusters. The editors, Kalle Lasn and Micah White, sent out a longer email to their 90,000 members to explain the thinking.

The email was headed with an image of a ballet dancer posing atop the Wall Street bull. Referencing the early optimism of the Arab Spring and the occupation of Tahrir Square, the text talked about the power of manifold voices uniting behind a single demand: "We zero in on what our one demand will be, a demand that awakens the imagination and, if achieved, would propel us toward the radical democracy of the future… and then we go out and seize a square of singular symbolic significance and put our asses on the line to make it happen." This time, the target would be "the greatest corruptor of our democracy: Wall Street, the financial Gomorrah of America".

As for the demand: "The most exciting candidate that we've heard so far is one that gets at the core of why the American political establishment is currently unworthy of being called a democracy: we demand that Barack Obama ordain a Presidential Commission tasked with ending the influence money has over our representatives in Washington. It's time for REPRESENTATION NOT CORPORATION."

The hope was that a continued occupation of Wall Street would force the government "to choose publicly between the will of the people and the lucre of the corporations". As well as a presidential commission on separating money from politics, this would involve the reinstatement of the Glass-Steagall Act (introduced by Roosevelt to separate commercial and investment banking, in a way that might have helped prevent the crisis of 2008 had it not been repealed) and a 'three strikes and you're out' law for corporate criminals.

You don't have to be a radical anti-consumerist or anti-capitalist to see something in the anti-corporate spirit of the Occupy Wall Street movement, or to appreciate how thoroughly it was lost in the decade that followed. The anger was about the corporatisation of politics. But what came next was its flipside: the politicisation of corporations. 'Representation not corporation' was the cry. But by 2020 it had become 'representation *by* corporation'. We've seen how it played out, symbolised by the exit of the ballet dancer and the arrival of Fearless Girl, the statue commissioned by State Street as a superficial symbol of feminist protest. And we've seen the consequences, from weaker marketing to worse social outcomes.

The answer starts with reasserting the difference between representation and corporation, and relearning why the separation of business and politics always mattered, and matters even more now. The for-profit and not-for-profit distinction remains fundamental, and purpose definitionally blurs the line.

In case that sounds too abstract, let's ground it in the story of two business people who wanted to do some good in the world, but went about it in different ways. I consider one of them a spirit guide for the road away from hell. And it's not the one with the hiking gear; it's the one with the salad dressing.

Patagonia goes purpose

"Billionaire No More: Patagonia Founder Gives Away the Company" said the New York Times headline on 14 September 2022. 50 years after founding his company, it was reported that former mountaineer and reluctant billionaire Yvon Chouinard would be giving away his fortune, in a move he described not as "going public", but "going purpose".

There is plenty to like about Yvon Chouinard. Californian son of French-Canadian parents, he was a misfit at school who found his niche in the Falconry Club, rappelling down cliffs in search of hawks' nests. After a stint in his brother's private detective agency, he taught himself blacksmithing in order to make his own climbing equipment, which he began to sell to friends. But his commercial breakthrough came with a trip to Scotland, where the rugby shirts caught his eye and he began to sell them back home. From these small beginnings, an apparel enterprise grew, always with a focus on sustainability and a wariness of commercial success. "I've been a businessman for almost sixty years," Chouinard wrote in 2006. "It's as difficult for me to say those words as it is for someone to admit being an alcoholic or a lawyer."

Chouinard has been hailed as a hero by advocates of corporate purpose, but he is not always keen to return the compliment. In an open letter announcing the "going purpose" move, he dealt a veiled but deadly blow to the movement:

"One option was to sell Patagonia and donate all the money," Chouinard explains in the letter. "But we couldn't be sure a new owner would maintain our values or keep our team of people around the world employed." Then comes the death blow: "Another path was to take the company public. What a disaster that would have been. Even public companies with good intentions are under too much pressure to create short-term gain at the expense of long-term vitality and responsibility."

Here, Chouinard expresses the view that would have purpose critics denounced as pessimists and cynics in any other context. Even public companies with good intentions can't be truly purposeful, and the very attempt would be a disaster. So all those 'start with why' narratives, all those US Business Roundtable pledges, all the Unilevers, Danones, Metas, BlackRocks and P&Gs… all of them are written off by the prophet of purpose, even while most hailed him as their saviour.

Meanwhile, Patagonia had long wrestled with its own internal tensions. The honest activism of its leader existed alongside a natural self-publicising instinct: a tendency towards grand branding gestures that saw the contradictions writ large.

As a piece of advertising history, the 'Don't buy this jacket' ad from 2011 is hard to beat. Published on Black Friday, it was heralded as a business finally doing the right thing and telling its customers to consume less. "We ask you to buy less and to reflect before you spend a dime on this jacket or anything else," said the copy, setting out the environmental cost of each jacket that came off the production line. "As is true of all the things we can make and you can buy, this jacket comes with an environmental cost higher than its price," continued the copy. "Don't buy what you don't need. Think twice before you buy anything."

The explicit message was clear. But anyone with any marketing instinct knows that a full-page ad in the New York Times on Black Friday, complete with a logo and product shot, written in a way that is designed to generate attention and positive PR, is going to do what ads tend to do. Patagonia's sales reportedly rose 30% in the nine months following the ad.[107] Philosophy students can discuss whether it therefore 'worked'.

The same tendency towards self-publicity was evident in the fanfare around the new business structure. "Earth is now our only shareholder," said the headline. "Instead of 'going public', you could say we're 'going purpose'" said the press release. It's a smart line, but a strange one for Chouinard, who is so clearly aware of the delusions in the wider purpose movement. You might think he wouldn't want to fan the flames of that fire. Yet many purpose advocates in the multinational corporate world saw it as validation of their movement. Like much of what Patagonia does, you could describe it as good PR, but bad activism. A more radical approach might have been to distance Patagonia from a corporate movement that sets back the cause of real environmental action. But that would be less popular among business readers who buy high-performance jackets for the arduous walk from the front door to the Tesla.

Meanwhile, criticism began to emerge of the 'giving away the company' story that was framed in quasi-saintly terms by the New York Times. The details of the new structure told a more complex story.

Chouinard had announced the transfer of the entire voting stock (representing 2% of the value of the company) to the

Patagonia Purpose Trust, created to uphold the values of the business. The non-voting stock (representing 98% of the value of the company) would go to the Holdfast Collective, a new non-profit "dedicated to fighting the environmental crisis and defending nature". Each year, Patagonia would keep enough profits to cover its operating costs, while handing the rest to the Holdfast Collective, which would use the money "to fight the environmental crisis, protect nature and biodiversity, and support thriving communities". Significantly, the Holdfast Collective is recognised as tax-exempt under the US Internal Revenue code 501(c)(4)—which means that, unlike public charities, it is legally allowed to engage in political activity. As estate attorney Matthew Erskine pointed out in Forbes, "the only one who loses will be the government, since if the entire $3 billion value of the company was taxable Chouinard's estate would owe $1.6 billion, or more if after 2025, in federal estate taxes".[108]

As commentators noted, there was a recent parallel for this move. A few weeks earlier, the New York Times reported on Barre Seid, the right-wing billionaire who handed his company over to a conservative non-profit organisation, which immediately sold it to generate $1.6 billion to spend on conservative causes—including fighting action on climate change.[109] The move was reported as an example of 'dark money' influencing politics: a billionaire converting his market power into long-term political influence. Patagonia can reasonably claim to be less dark—there is no mystery about where the money is coming from, although there will be limited transparency on where it's going. But it's part of the same trend for private interests weighing in on the political process.

Professor Carl Rhodes, a notable left-of-centre critic of purpose, has examined why this is worth worrying about:

> "We live in an era in which business owners are taking over as society's moral arbiters, using their wealth to address what they see as society's greatest problems. Meanwhile, the wealth and number of the world's billionaires grows, and inequality stretches society to breaking point. It is great that Chouinard is putting his company to work for the future of the planet. What is not great is how our lives and our futures are increasingly dependent on the power and generosity of the rich elite, rather than ruled by the common will of the people."[110]

Other left-wing critics have been more fiery. Comedian and political commentator Adam Conover made a memorable film eviscerating both Patagonia and the media for spinning such a feel-good story: "Not only was this a donation to help Chouinard avoid billions of dollars in taxes," he argues, "but the fact that it's even possible for a billionaire to pull this maneuver is an unmitigated disaster for the planet and for our democracy." Conover points out how Chouinard could have sustained the avowed purpose of the company by transferring his $3 billion worth of shares to his children, who could have kept running it according to his wishes—but this was the move that would have generated over a billion in taxes.

Instead, the novel arrangement ensured the family retained effective control over the commercial operations, while holding the purse strings to the Holdfast Collective, which would exert political influence in perpetuity. "Yvon was able to take his $3 billion company and turn it into a $3 billion political influence machine, tax free," continues Conover. "He didn't pay capital gains tax on the growth of the company, he didn't pay the income tax that I would have to pay before I donate to my favourite 501(c)(4), and he definitely didn't pay the gift taxes you normally have to pay if you want to give $3 billion in money and political influence to your kids." He concludes: "Because of their control over Patagonia and Holdfast, Chouinard's descendants are going to wield massive political power for their entire lives. They're going to be invited to meetings with powerful elected leaders. They'll be flown around the world to conferences. They'll be lauded as great philanthropists until the day they die, when their kids will take over… Chouinard has turned his money into permanent political power for him and his descendants, and I do not think he should get a tax break for doing it."

Conover concedes that the intentions behind this may be good, and there may be limited social benefits from this instance. But the wider point is systemic: do we want to enable and encourage these arrangements for the Barre Seids as well as the Yvon Chouinards, and do we want to live in a society where the democratic process is influenced even more by private money than it has been in the past? Yes, the left can cheer on the billionaires on its own side of the political divide. But it's all a long way from the 'representation not corporation' spirit of Occupy Wall Street.

A better strategy, both short and long-term, might be to

cheer on another kind of hero. And we could do worse than choose Paul Newman.

Newman goes human

If you'd visited Paul Newman's Connecticut house around December 1980, you might have expected to find a Hollywood star sitting by the fire, telling tales about starring in The Hustler, Butch Cassidy and the Sundance Kid, or Cool Hand Luke. Alternatively, you might have expected to find this part-time racecar enthusiast and four time national championship winner hunched over an engine in the garage. Instead, you would have been directed into the basement to be confronted by a man stirring a giant bathtub of olive oil with a wooden rowing paddle, pausing only to take swigs of Budweiser and instruct his friend and neighbour, the writer A.E. Hotchner, to pour in another jar of mustard.

Paul Newman liked salad dressing. In high-end restaurants, he would ask waiters to hold back the dressing and instead bring the ingredients for him to mix his own. When one restaurant served pre-dressed salad, he quietly took it to the bathroom to wash it down, patted it dry with kitchen towel, then set about work on his dressing. At the time, most dressings contained sugar, artificial colouring and chemical preservatives—Newman preferred the taste and wholesomeness of his own.

Newman was an independent thinker in other areas of

life. In his early acting years, he rejected advice to change his Jewish surname and instead embraced the Jewish side of his identity "because it's more of a challenge". A lifelong Democrat, he attended the March on Washington in 1962, was present at the first Earth Day in 1970, became a vocal supporter of gay rights and same-sex marriage, and listed his proudest achievement as appearing at no.19 on Richard Nixon's 'enemies list', which was made public during the Watergate hearings.

Newman's friend and neighbour A.E. Hotchner was a novelist, playwright and biographer of Ernest Hemingway, with whom he enjoyed a close friendship. Now Hotchner and Newman were plotting a new venture: entering the salad dressing business. It began as a joke, born of Newman's obsessive interest in the product. But soon it took on a momentum of its own. Newman and Hotchner struck supply and distribution deals, poring over every detail of the contracts to ensure product quality would be maintained. Newman was reluctantly persuaded to put his face on the product packaging, which he saw as crass but commercially necessary. The partners compensated by using the rest of the packaging for witty copy that communicated a brand not taking itself too seriously. The proud slogan on the first bottles of dressing read: "Newman's Own. Fine foods since February", while the back labels contained an outlandish and entirely fabricated origin story specific to each product. These days, inane copy on supermarket packaging is the norm. Back then, it was a different way to build a brand without the need for more costly advertising.

From the outset, Newman was clear that he didn't care

about making money. "There probably won't be any profits," he said to his partner. "But if there are, how about we give everything we make to charity?" As the business grew, those profits became significant, and an unusual organisational structure developed. Newman's Own was a commercial venture, gradually expanding its range to include pizzas, coffee, fruit juices and more. The business kept just enough money to cover its operating costs, but started each new financial year at zero, giving 100% of the profits to its non-profit partner, the Newman's Own Foundation.

Initially, the proceeds were given as grants to various community organisations, but Newman and Hotchner became interested in setting up their own projects, including residential summer camps for terminally ill children: giving them the chance to share a joyful experience with children in a similar predicament, while surrounded by trained carers and access to advanced medical facilities. In the early years, Newman and Hotchner played an active role, helping to build the camps, recruit the staff and navigate the associated red tape. The idea became a phenomenon that spread around the world. Now the camps operate across five continents and over 1.5 million camping experiences have been provided to children and families free of charge. Other projects include FoodCorps, promoting healthy food in schools, and Indigenous Food Justice, reviving culinary traditions in marginalised communities. To date, more than $600 million has been invested in charitable work—more than Newman might have imagined in that Connecticut basement.

You might see this as an inspirational tale of purpose before its time. But purpose would be the exact wrong way to frame it. "I really cannot lay claim to some terribly philanthropic instinct in my base nature," said Paul Newman of the venture. "It was just a combination of circumstances. If the business had stayed small and had just been in three local stores, it would never have gone charitable. It was an abhorrence of combining tackiness, exploitation, and putting money in my pocket, which was excessive in every direction." Describing the subsequent idea for the camps, Newman says: "I'd be pleased if I could announce a motive of lofty purpose. I've been accused of compassion, of altruism, of devotion to Christian, Hebrew, and Moslem ethic, but however desperate I am to claim ownership of a high ideal, I cannot."

Like most successful entrepreneurs, Newman didn't start with why, but with an obsessive focus on the what. Under pressure to cut corners in production, Newman and Hotchner held their ground and researched ways to make the product both natural and commercially viable. Early buyers from the big chains paid tribute to this single-minded product focus: "The dressing's success rests not in Mr. Newman's name or the company's non-profit status, but in the taste. It's different from other salad dressings and it's high quality. People buy it for the same reason they buy other products. They like it."[111]

Nevertheless, what you might call a 'why' gradually emerged for Newman and Hotchner: the kind of 'why' that might only make sense in retrospect. The humour in their work went deeper than the packaging copy: it was a way of thinking about business, and about life. They were keen to acknowledge the role of luck and happenstance. There was a lightness of touch that is entirely absent from the po-faced businesses of the purpose movement. You would never catch Paul Newman doing what Yvon Chouinard is filmed doing on the Patagonia website: handwriting 'Earth is now our only shareholder' before gazing meaningfully out of the window. Newman had too keen a sense of irony for that, even though he had more claim than anyone to doing direct, hands-on work for good.

The story is related by A.E. Hotchner in a book titled Shameless Exploitation in Pursuit of the Common Good—Newman's playful phrase that captured the two sides of the operation. Originally published in 2003, the book was re-released in 2008, around the time of Newman's death, aged 83. Sadly, the title was sanitised for the purpose age. Now it was just In Pursuit of the Common Good—an act of editing that loses the knowing humour of the brand. As is often the case with business successions, attempts to extend Newman's legacy have had mixed results, and Newman's daughter has complained of being pressured and marginalised by management in the years that followed. Nevertheless, Newman's Own remains a notable outlier in the field of business and philanthropy. In 2018, its unusual structure led to the Newman's Own Exception being written into law by Congress: a narrow exception created after some unease about whether this unusual alliance of for-profit and non-profit organisations might be used as a way around corporate tax law.[112]

In the 2022 coverage of Patagonia 'going purpose', some commentators noted the parallel with Newman's Own, which got there four decades earlier. But there is a crucial difference. The Newman's Own structure contains a clear separation of church and state, or more accurately of for-profit and not-for-profit. The charitable side is a separate entity run by sector experts who know what they're doing, while the business side is run by product and marketing people who know what they're doing. There is no pretence that every marketing campaign is somehow a campaign for good: Paul Newman reluctantly recognised the need to tell customers that 100% of profits went to charity, but he was instinctively against what he called "noisy philanthropy". In the same way that using his own image for profit felt tacky, the idea of leveraging the good cause as a marketing tool felt equally tacky. He never lost sight of the founding logic: he was doing this because he had an intense interest in salad dressing. The philanthropy was an unexpected by-product. As he describes it, the venture began as a joke, but turned into "a very practical joke".

This was more than a difference in attitude: it was a difference in legal status. The Newman's Own Foundation is a 501(c)(3) organisation whose tax-exempt status requires it *not* to fund political candidates or lobby for legislative change. Patagonia is pointedly different: it is explicitly set up to intervene in the democratic process. And it's this blurring of church and state that is at the heart of the problem. However favourably you look on individual cases, it's a disturbing pattern to endorse and reinforce.

The difference in the Newman's Own approach is that it foregrounds the divide that purposeful business seeks to erase. It's not the salad dressings that are purposeful, and there is no pretence that the business itself is a heroic actor. In law and in spirit, the operation respects the divide that society asserts. Purposeful businesses seek to blur it, both to others and to themselves, and it leads to a deep form of cognitive dissonance.

It's no coincidence that this surfaces in the manner of the people involved. When you read about Yvon Chouinard, as with other purposeful players like Paul Polman and Alan Jope at Unilever, or Larry Fink at BlackRock, there is a perpetual sense of earnestness and solemnity about the enterprise. You rarely see much humour or levity. Chouinard appears agonised by his own success. He stares thoughtfully out of windows. He is like the Chief Executives around the US Business Roundtable, comparing themselves to Thomas Jefferson. Purpose invites an elevated sense of your own self-worth, combined with a sense of frustration at the internal contradictions.

In contrast, the original incarnation of Newman's Own strikes me as a fun place to be, alive with wit and humour, and a healthy sense of humility. This is not to say that the current incarnation of Newman's Own has hit on an operational structure that can finally make a success of purpose. As the Newman's Own Exception suggests, it's an unusual structure that might be open to abuse if used more widely. And, as the changing of the book title suggests, Newman's Own no longer has the lightness of touch that defined its early years.

But this points to a deeper truth about business. Throughout their years in partnership, Newman and Hotchner were perpetually fighting against the grain of their own creation. The business was a machine full of inbuilt incentives towards 'shameless exploitation', and they did their best at every turn to ensure it retained its founding spirit, both in terms of how the products were made and how the profits were invested. They brought humour and humility to the work, along with an essential humanity. The business wasn't purposeful, but they eventually discovered that they were. That might be a better way to think about purpose in general: as something that resides in people, not corporations.

The road away from hubris

The aim of the next three sections is not to cut the red tape on the grand opening of the road to heaven. But it is to offer three signposts pointing roughly in the right direction: humour, humility and humanity. If you're a marketer managing a brand, an agency creating a campaign, or a CEO managing a business, I suggest they're three useful reference points for every decision you make.

All three point in the opposite direction to the signature word of the purpose movement: hubris. And it's worth a brief diversion to Etymology Corner to discover what hubris means.

Most readers will be familiar with the everyday sense of excessive pride or arrogance. 'Arrogance' itself is an interesting word, coming from the Latin *adrogare*, meaning to feel one 'has the right to demand certain attitudes or behaviours'. To arrogate means to claim or seize without justification, or to make undue claims to possessing.

Hubris is Greek in origin. Like arrogance, it is associated

with the overstepping of boundaries. In classical Greek tragedy, hubris is often the fatal shortcoming than brings about the fall of the tragic hero. Typically, overconfidence leads the hero to attempt to overstep the boundaries of human limitations and assume a godlike status. Even for gods, this was a bad move. The Greeks believed the Fates had assigned each being a particular area of freedom, which the gods themselves could not breach. Hubris referred to the breaching of those limits, and it took on a specific meaning in everyday law, referring to transgressive crimes of assault and theft of public property. In the New Testament, hubris parallels the Hebrew word *pasha*, meaning transgression. It represents an overweening pride that causes man to defy God, sometimes to the degree that he considers himself an equal.

You might see where I'm going with this. At root, corporate purpose is about the overstepping of a societal boundary. It is limited companies, sometimes with sincerely held good intentions, choosing to step beyond their limited remit and tackle broader societal questions. At its most banal, it is mayonnaise with a purpose, or Pepsi approaching the police line. But at the more systemic level, it is BlackRock using trillions of money that it does not own to push an agenda for which no one voted. It is Facebook saying we give people 'the power to build community and bring the world closer together', while systemically boosting polarisation and tribal politics. It is Spotify saying it 'unlocks the potential of human creativity' while musicians struggle more than ever. It is the CEO of Johnson & Johnson saying he feels like Thomas Jefferson.

The crossing of the boundary was written into the

purpose movement from the start. It encouraged brands and leaders to claim a higher social mission that went beyond the conventional, lower-case-p purpose that businesses had always possessed. This definitional hubris inevitably surfaces in the everyday actions of businesses and brands. You see it in the CEOs expressing political views on behalf of their employees, the CMOs talking about being on the right side of history at Cannes, the soap brand putting its logo on the face of Covid nurses, the chocolate company claiming an award for 'social purpose' on the back of years of tax avoidance. Hubris is the crossing of the divide between for-profit and not-for-profit, private and public, commercial and political.

The signposts of humour, humility and humanity point in another direction.

Humour is serious business

In 1970, London design agency Crosby Fletcher Forbes created a poster in support of the Campaign Against Museum Admission Charges. It was protesting the Conservative government's plan to end free admission to 18 national museums and galleries across the UK. Consisting solely of plain text, the poster read: "We, the undersigned, deplore and oppose the Government's intention to introduce admission charges to national museums and galleries." Underneath was a series of handwritten signatures. After a moment for the penny to drop, you realise they are the familiar signatures of Van Gogh, Rembrandt, Bruegel, Titian and other artists.

It was a witty idea in service of a serious cause, making the point that artists need wide audiences just as much as wide audiences need access to our shared heritage. But, like a lot of design and advertising, the poster made no obvious impact. The government went ahead and introduced the charges anyway, and observers at the time might have concluded that clever design ideas are all very well, but don't really get you anywhere.

Three decades later, Labour minister Chris Smith reversed the policy, reinstating free entry to the museums. In an interview with the Guardian, he talked about his inspiration: "I remember as a student being struck by a poster arguing against museum charges," he explained. "It said: 'We the undersigned oppose the introduction of admission charges' and carried the signatures of Van Gogh, Turner and other great artists. It made me realise a simple truth: that free admission is all about giving everyone, no matter what their means, the chance to see the greatest works of art, science and history that our nation has."[113]

The poster wasn't credited by name in the Guardian article, but it rang a bell and I tracked it down to a 1997 book called A Smile in the Mind: Witty Thinking in Graphic Design. All these years later, Chris Smith was referencing a poster that had been designed in 1970, earned itself a small place in a design book, and otherwise been consigned to design history. Of course, it would be an exaggeration to say the poster led directly to the policy change. But the fact that it could stay in the mind of a future government minister for three decades, to the point where he could describe it in detail, is testament to the power of witty thinking to make a lasting impression.

Wit and humour have had a tough time in the purpose era. Kantar research suggests a decline in humorous advertising that set in around 2009 and only began to recover around 2022.[114] You might see this as an appropriate response to serious times—the austerity decade, the rise of Trump and Brexit, and the arrival of Covid. If so, you would be disagreeing with a large swathe of the public. The same Kantar research suggests people still wanted to see humour in advertising, and indeed wanted it more than ever during the pandemic. After all, there had been serious times before— the 1970s weren't exactly a barrel of laughs. Or rather they were, because humorous advertising continued to entertain and engage people. Humour can be a sane response to hard times.

The real reason for the decline in humour was the corresponding rise of purposeful advertising. Humour tends to poke fun at the powerful and prick the bubbles of the proud. It doesn't sit well with grand statements about making the world a better place. Indeed, humour's main place during the purpose era has been as an act of resistance. If there's one silver lining to purpose, it's the satirical sketches it has inspired.

One of them is 'Left-Handed Mango Chutney'. It starts with an advertiser at a dinner party, proudly talking about creating an 'innovation piece' for a local mango chutney company. He explains that the product is aimed at the left-handed community ("the planner really helped beef up the case by playing on how the left-handed community is under-represented"). The other guests hesitantly ask if it's available in shops. "No… it was more of a limited run," says the adman. "How many did you sell, Greg?" asks one guest. "Six," answers Greg, "…but we generated 12 billion impressions and helped build brand engagement by 112 per cent. We also won the Grand Prix." After a long, awkward silence, another guest pipes up: "I actually also work in advertising." "And what… case studies have you done?" asks one guest wearily. "I wrote the beer ad where the horse farts," she replies. "Oh yeah!" reply the delighted guests. "I saw that one! That went viral!" A bemused Greg looks around as the table dissolves into laughter and animated discussion.[115]

People used to laugh at ads; now they laugh at ad agencies. I wrote that in 2021 and unfortunately it remains true now. But the mango chutney sketch also makes a serious point. Ask anyone to name their favourite ads from over the years, and the chances are that humour will feature prominently. It could be 'The Man Your Man Could Smell Like' for Old Spice, or the 'Whassup' ads for Budweiser, or the Super Bowl-dominating 'It's a Tide ad' from 2019. It might be Peter Kay's 'top bombing' for John Smith's, 'I'm a Mac, I'm a PC' for Apple, or the Hamlet and Heineken ads from decades gone by. All are funny, but all were seriously successful answers to high-stakes commercial briefs.

Other examples of humour might not be laugh-out-loud funny, but involve gentle wit or a lateral leap. Many are contained in A Smile in the Mind, the book I mentioned above, which I was involved in updating in 2016. Flick through its pages and you'll discover how many of your favourite brands contain a hidden smile: the arrow in the FedEx logo, the bear in the Toblerone logo, the daily variations on the Google logo, the smile linking the A and Z of the Amazon logo. Wit can work for big brands, small brands, commercial brands and charitable causes. It's not the only way to do successful advertising and branding, but it's often the key that unlocks a communication challenge. Wit builds a connection between two separate points, tying a knot between two threads of thought. That creates a similar moment of connection in the mind of the recipient.

"Laughter is the shortest distance between two people," said Victor Borge. This is the social purpose that is written into humour itself. It cuts through and connects. A Biden and Trump supporter might never agree on politics, but they can both laugh at the same joke. And if one can make the other laugh, it's a glimmer of shared humanity: a meaningful connection that might lead to better conversations.

Not all advertising needs to be funny, but all ad agencies, and ideally all business people, should do their best to maintain a sense of humour. Even in serious times, it stops you becoming too carried away by your importance, or too earnestly wrapped up in your own heroic narrative. It's psychologically healthier too. Paul Newman retained a sense of ironic detachment from his work, even though it meant a lot to him. In contrast, purposeful people often seem less than happy with life: there's an uptightness that comes with the uprightness. Tortured logic leads to tortured minds. At the end of the day, you're selling gilets and mayonnaise. It helps to remember that.

Humility beats hubris

'Nobody's perfect' said the headline on one of the classic Volkswagen ads from the 1960s. The image showed a Beetle with a flat tyre, and the text talked about Volkswagen's service department, which exists because even the most reliable cars have issues. It's not often you see humility in advertising, but if you get it right, it exudes a kind of confidence: not humble-bragging exactly, but a sense of not having to exaggerate because the reality is impressive enough.

Like many great ads of the time, it was created by Bill Bernbach, the adman whom we've met in these pages before. He's the one who said 'A principle isn't a principle until it costs you something.' Maybe it's going too far to say he's the patron saint of the post-purpose era, if and when it comes. But there is inspiration to be found in his life and career, which is related in a biography by Doris Willens. Its title, appropriately, is Nobody's Perfect.

Born and raised in the Bronx, Bernbach got his first break while working in the mailroom of Schenley Distillers. He took the initiative to write an ad for Schenley's American Cream Whiskey, managed to get it in front of the right people, and was promoted to the advertising department. After stints in a couple of agencies, he grew disenchanted with the sameness and safeness of the work. In a precocious letter to his bosses at Grey, he made an appeal for creativity over conformity: "It's that creative spark that I'm so jealous of for our agency and that I am so desperately fearful of losing. I don't want academicians. I don't want scientists. I don't want people who do the right things. I want people who do inspiring things." The letter ended: "Let us blaze new trails. Let us prove to the world that good taste, good art, and good writing can be good selling."

Bernbach ended up blazing a trail of his own, leaving Grey to start up Doyle Dane Bernbach, which would produce much of the witty, conceptual, ideas-based work of the 1960s. Avis made a strength of its perpetual second place in the market by saying 'We try harder'. Volkswagen became the Duchamp of the car advertising world, with surreal headlines like 'Lemon' and 'Think small', introducing charmingly persuasive, product-driven copy. Bernbach didn't write the ads himself, but he created the agency culture that produced them, popularising the writer-art director teams that would become the norm in decades to come.

Like most decent people in the days before purpose, Bill Bernbach didn't see advertising as an ethics-free zone. From the start, the agency was wary of getting involved in political advertising, seeing democracy as a different realm to commerce, and not one for the slick persuaders of Madison Avenue. But the Republican candidacy of Barry Goldwater in 1964 sparked Trump-like fears of right-wing extremism and a slide towards nuclear war. DDB was the agency of the moment and ended up taking the Democrat brief, working for incumbent Lyndon Johnson.

The result was one of the most remembered political ads of all time: 'Daisy'. Until 1964, campaign ads were usually information-rich and positively focused on the campaigning candidate, rather than attacking the opponent. 'Daisy' contained almost zero policy and few words. Instead, it opens with a little girl in a meadow, plucking the petals from a daisy.

She counts them aloud and makes a few charming mistakes: one, two, three, four… seven, six… six, eight, nine… Then the film freezes and a nuclear countdown commences in a stern male voice: Ten, nine, eight, seven… At zero, a mushroom cloud explodes with devastating force. "These are the stakes," says the voice of Lyndon Johnson. "To make a world in which all of God's children can live. Or to go into the dark. We must either love each other, or we must die." Then the endline: "Vote for President Johnson on November 3rd. The stakes are too high for you to stay home."

The ad aired only once, at a time when the polls were already swinging towards Johnson, who won in a landslide victory. Nevertheless, it caused an impact, generating reams of press coverage and angering Republicans who saw it as overstepping a line: deliberately frightening voters with irresponsible scare stories. At the time, Bernbach may have seen it as a battle worth fighting: something that captured the mood and consolidated the growing sentiment against Goldwater. But in later years, Bernbach would be haunted by the ad's legacy. It became known as the first ever political attack ad, and the advertising arms race has escalated ever since—often with the Republicans landing the more powerful blows.

There were no doubt times when Bernbach pondered the ethics of that decision. But his most successful years in advertising coincided with the rise of another issue: tobacco. In a 1971 interview with the Los Angeles Times, Bernbach discussed his agency's voluntary anti-tobacco stance, which had been in place since the US Surgeon General published an influential report about the dangers of smoking in 1964.

"We were never on a crusade," Bernbach is quoted as saying. "We just didn't want to be responsible. It was a matter of principle and it cost us money—cigarette advertising is the most profitable kind you can have." Then comes the quote that has become particularly resonant in the purpose age: "But I don't feel a principle is a principle until it costs you money."[116]

It's a powerful turn of phrase—the kind of thing you might expect from a great adman who is making a persuasive pitch for his agency in the pages of the LA Times, where potential clients will be reading with interest. But note the disclaimer: "We were never on a crusade." Bernbach's instinct is not to set himself up as a moral hero. After all, his first copywriting breakthrough had come with a whisky ad, which was viewed more sternly back then than it is now. For many years, liquor companies effectively chose to ban themselves from the powerful new media of television and radio. Fearing the return of Prohibition if America developed too big a drinking problem, the companies decided it was better to stay under the radar and play the long game. It was only in the 1990s that things changed, by which time, cigarette advertising was already history.

Bernbach's moral modesty was also appropriate, because the sacrifice involved in cases like these is complex. Ad agencies are set up to handle a finite amount of work, so the act of turning away business is not necessarily a real-terms loss, especially for agencies like DDB who are in high demand. In pure ethical terms, there is also a distinction between an actual cost, in the sense of losing money you have now, and a theoretical cost, in the sense of foregoing potential future income over and above what you will continue to make. Both costs matter, but only one leaves you going home poorer, maybe to a smaller house. In terms of strict business calculation, you could read DDB's stance as a case of enlightened self-interest. The Surgeon General's report had already made clear which way the wind was blowing, so any agency reliant on tobacco advertising was perilously exposed. Much better to get out in front of the inevitable and turn it into a positive PR story—the kind of thing that gets the interest of LA Times journalists, and which might lead to more lucrative, long-term work elsewhere.

None of which is to succumb to cynicism, but simply to weigh the ethical and practical considerations honestly. Similar quandaries arise now for agencies uncomfortable with advertising airlines or oil companies. Some might look back and see Bernbach as a moral hero, purposeful before his time, nobly making the sacrifice that others should be making now. But there's another lesson that can be drawn from the story. You see it partly in the tone of the interview. There's no sense of pomposity or self-righteously shaming the agencies who do otherwise. And five years after the interview was published, there was an interesting and melancholy coda.

Bernbach chose to step down from his Chief Executive role in 1976, remaining in an Honorary Chairman role, but passing the baton to a new management team. When Bernbach died in 1982, the management proceeded with unseemly haste to end the agency's ban on tobacco advertising and take on the Parliament cigarette account—a small account in itself, but a foot in the door of Philip Morris, owner of major alcohol and soft drinks brands as well as tobacco, and the world's fourth biggest advertiser at the time. The story was significant enough to be reported in the New York Times, which notes how a similar fate befell David Ogilvy, another great adman who chose to ban tobacco advertising based on personal conviction—a ban subsequently lifted by new management.[117]

Both stories can be seen as a depressing reflection on the industry. But there is another moral at their heart. As the New York Times article notes, Bernbach fully accepted the transfer of power when he stepped down as Chief Executive in 1976. His words at the time: "Look, you people are running the company now—you're going to have to make up your own minds."

As it happened, the new owners made up their minds to follow the money, although they chose to retain a ban on political advertising, which Doyle Dane Bernbach had restored following the 1964 campaign, perhaps realising the Pandora's box they had opened.

For the purposes of this chapter, Bernbach's words point to something significant. He was a man with ethical convictions, but he also had the humility to recognise the distinction between himself and the company. There was no attempt to lock DDB into his own ethical worldview in perpetuity. Years before his death, Bernbach had himself appeared willing to waive the tobacco principle when it threatened a potentially lucrative merger with ad agency FCB, owner of large tobacco accounts. "I've turned the agency over to a new group of people and they are responsible for its destiny, its wellbeing," said Bernbach. "They can't be slaves to a decision I made nearly 20 years before this." So even Bernbach's principles had their price: the merger would have secured the financial future of his family, at a time when he was already quietly suffering from the leukaemia that would kill him.

For Bernbach, there had never been any pretence at being uniquely qualified to lead a grand moral crusade. His views about tobacco were his views, and his agency was successful enough that he could safely implement them without risking the incomes or job security of his staff. Either way, the moral stance reflected his values, not the supposed 'values' of DDB as a corporate entity. Once he was gone, it was up to other people.

Humility might seem an odd value to promote in the advertising world. The last thing I'd want to see would be a wave of falsely humble-bragging ads or marketers taking to the Cannes stage to talk bashfully about how they're just doing their best and shucks, if it leads to a few purpose awards, then great. But I see humility as a useful touchstone for brands when they're developing campaigns, and for CEOs when they're pondering the role of their company in the world. Purpose asks you to start with why, define your higher societal mission, then lead the global conversation. Humility asks you to take it down a notch. Correctly defined, it's not about self-deprecation or falsely talking yourself down: it's etymologically related to the idea of being grounded and in touch with reality. A state between self-aggrandisement and self-deprecation, humility is considered one of the great virtues in the Abrahamic religions, and is close to the idea of being 'unselved' in Buddhism. To quote the phrase usually attributed to C.S. Lewis, it's not about thinking less of yourself, but thinking of yourself less.

How does that translate into day-to-day decision-making? Well, look at any ad you're doing—are you making yourself the hero in this story? Why not make it more about the customer? Or look at any keynote speech you're giving—are you talking like the leader of a social movement? Are you equating yourself with the business? Are you speaking on behalf of your employees about social issues? Why not listen more than talk? It can be a useful exercise to look in the mirror and think, "Look, I'm only making ads" or "I'm only selling soap"—not as something reductive, but as a way of staying grounded, which ultimately projects strength. Humility is the antidote to hubris.

Humanity, unlimited

In July 2023, a Canadian academic claimed to have identified the only known example of Geoffrey Chaucer's handwriting. The writer of The Canterbury Tales worked for 12 years as controller of the London Wool Quay, filing paperwork to ensure King Richard II was receiving his share of tax from each trade. Professor Richard Green of Ohio State University claims a scribbled note dating from this period (1374 to 1386) is written in Chaucer's own hand. What does this one surviving fragment from the hand of the great poet say? Chaucer was asking for time off work.[118]

Chaucer wasn't the only poet to hold down a less glamorous day job. Philip Larkin was a librarian. T.S. Eliot was a banker. Maya Angelou was a streetcar conductor. Robert Burns was a tax collector. In other art forms, Philip Glass was a plumber and taxi driver. Toni Morrison was an editor. Charlotte Bronte was a governess. George Bernard Shaw worked for the Edison telephone company. Kurt Vonnegut managed a Saab dealership. Vivian Maier was a nanny. Jeff Koons was a commodities broker.

I mention all this because it points to an obvious truth: work isn't everything. You don't have to be a poet or painter to find that your main passion, and your main sense of purpose, lies outside work. You might love to travel. You might love playing sport. You might find deep meaning in raising children, or looking after ageing parents. You might go to church every Sunday, or the match every Saturday. You might be in a band, learning to knit, going to dance classes, or volunteering in a soup kitchen. You might love going to the pub, or love going to museums. You might enjoy reading, immersing yourself in the words that Larkin, Angelou and Chaucer wrote on their days off.

Businesses can be powerful engines to drive all of those things—just by being businesses. It's entertaining to imagine a Chaucer or Koons reading the 'We're here to make the world a better place' purpose statements of their employers, and quietly thinking 'You're here to pay me—I've got plans of my own'.

That's not to say that work is a purely transactional relationship. There is nobility in labour, and it's what we spend many hours of our lives doing. So there's much to be said for having a job that you find tolerable and enjoyable, and an employer who doesn't make unreasonable demands.

The trouble is, purpose can often push against that. It frames business as an important social mission: important enough that maybe everyone should chip in and work this weekend, or maybe everyone should go along with it when their visionary, maverick boss is being slightly overbearing. The WeWorks and Theranoses of this world have thrived on the culture that purpose creates.

Others will find purpose in work more than anywhere else in life. It's undoubtedly true that a Steve Jobs or Anita Roddick might look back on their lives and consider work their defining achievement, just as a local plumber or window cleaner might find great meaning and satisfaction in their trade. To bring that point to life, here are the words of a window cleaner who worked on the World Trade Center in the years before 2001:

> "My world consists of windows and reflections. I prefer to be on the outside looking in. I'm the one who's free. Inside it's like a jail. I wouldn't ever want to change places with the big shots sitting inside in their leather chairs. As I pass their air-conditioned cages, I can see they'd love to rip off their ties. Me, I don't have any stress... It's pretty hellish up there when the wind whips around, though the cage is rock solid. But I've often come off the building with windburn. In summer there's a nice spidery breeze... But I love this job. I get $75 more than the window cleaners downstairs."[119]

Roko Camaj was on the roof of the south tower on September 11 2001 and his body was never found. His words come from a 1998 'Life in the Day' feature in the Sunday Times. As well as being hauntingly evocative, they are a poetic illustration of the role that work plays in many people's lives. Work can be a deeply meaningful thing, but that meaning is something we bring to it ourselves. It's not encoded in the top-down values of World Trade Center Window Cleaners plc, just as Chaucer's likely fascination with wool traders and London life wasn't part of the 'Golden Circle' of his employer.

When a Mark Zuckerberg or Howard Schultz looks around Facebook or Starbucks, they no doubt see a team of people all working towards a common purpose: 'to give people the power to build community and bring the world closer together', or 'to inspire and nurture the human spirit'. But I think it might be better, and truer, to look around and see something else: a group of people who all have purposes of their own. One might be a great poet, another a great mother. One might be a talented singer, another a committed activist. One might be a Republican, another a Democrat. As a business, you're powering all those things, most of which you'll never directly see for yourself. But by being a decent employer in a successful business, you're helping a lot of people to find meaning in their own lives.

The one way to spoil it is to start corralling people into a single world view. At this company, you're only allowed to talk politics if you're left of centre. At this company, you have to sign this DEI statement even if you see some bad as well as good in its world view. At this company, we believe in the one true vision and anyone who questions it is a naysayer, cynic or pessimist. At this company, we're here to make the world a better place, but we've already decided what 'better' means, and you need to get on board.

This distinction between corporate and human purpose is about more than poetry, art and finding a higher calling outside work: it's about human rights. In her 2024 book Higher Ground, Alison Taylor argues for human rights as an alternative ethical framework for corporations: "Putting human rights at the center of your values efforts is helpful because they focus on individual agency, bodily autonomy, and dignity—as opposed to imposing values on people who may not share them." This is a more radical and subversive idea than Taylor makes it sound. As she tactfully points out, "Human rights aren't corporate centric… they can act to counterbalance any tendency to place the company's interests at the center of the universe." Then the sign-off: "They raise important questions about the legitimacy (and limitations) of any corporate effort to exert political influence."

These questions were at the heart of a legal ruling that contributed to the rise of the purpose era. In the 2010 Citizens United vs Federal Election Committee ruling, the conservative-majority US Supreme Court came down on the side of corporations having the same constitutional rights as individual people—clearing the way for a flood of outside spending entering and influencing the election process.

Not all the increased spending came directly from corporations. The main outcome of the ruling was the creation of so-called Super PACs, which could accept unlimited contributions from individuals and corporations, so long as they didn't give any money directly to candidates. These groups have spent hundreds of millions on elections since they were first created in 2010. Elsewhere, there is the rise of so-called 'dark money' from non-profits, of the kind that Patagonia and the Holdfast Collective have since created. Such groups have even greater freedom to campaign on electoral issues, without disclosing the details of their donors.

All this goes to an essential issue at the heart of purpose. There are legal debates about the extent to which corporations are people. But the debate is an ethical and philosophical one too. Going back to the definitions of purpose with which this book began, you may remember that the secondary definition was about "a person's sense of resolve or determination". That sense is something a person can possess, but can the legal entity of a corporation really be imbued with that kind of purpose? Time and again, history shows how purposeful founders struggle to keep the spirit going in a way that outlasts them, and this is often seen as a source of frustration or even chronic depression, in the case of a Robert Owen or William Lever.

A healthier attitude might be to embrace the lack of control. Businesses are constrained in their capacity for delivering social change, because that's the way it should be. Purpose resides in humans, not companies. Businesses are limited; people aren't. When you accept that reality with grace and humility, you might be in a better position to do good within the necessary constraints of the system, without driving yourself to distraction by believing in a corporate utopia that can never exist.

Turning the telescope around

At this point, I imagine an attentive reader asking: humour, humility and humanity are all very well, but isn't this just another form of navel-gazing? Obsessing about your own internal nature, rather than the external world? What about turning the telescope around and looking in the other direction?

I'm glad I imagined that reader, because it's a good question.

In these closing sections, I want to focus on the marketing industry in particular, whose job ought to be helping clients look outwards, but whose ranks contain many early super-spreaders of the purpose meme. Many in adland now regard purpose as yesterday's news, having no idea how thoroughly purpose has embedded itself in the corporations and institutions that keep sending in the briefs. That myopia leads to some strange thinking around advertising and its place in the world.

"Today, politics is a category in decline, and currently Labour is the only party strategically and politically capable of emulating Sipsmith's achievements," wrote Saatchi & Saatchi chairman Richard Huntington in November 2023.[120] The article, which compared democratic politics to an artisan gin brand, appeared in the Independent, along with a front page splash saying "Thatcher's ad agency turns on 'cruel' Tories and backs Labour".

As the headline suggests, the association with the Saatchi name is what gave this intervention some weight. Maurice and Charles Saatchi will forever be associated with the 'Labour isn't working' poster that helped Margaret Thatcher to power in 1979—the headline accompanied by a photograph of a winding dole queue. In reality, the poster was a minor intervention that only became fabled in retrospect, but it was enough to build a long-standing relationship between Thatcher and the Saatchi brothers. One of her later public appearances was attending the Saatchi Gallery to celebrate the 40th anniversary of the founding of the agency.[121]

By then, the brothers had long since left to form M&C Saatchi in 1995. So you could say the act of using the Saatchi & Saatchi name to boost the 2023 pro-Labour intervention was akin to Bill Bernbach's agency taking on a tobacco account as soon as his back was turned: a lesson in how businesses outlast their founders and take a course far beyond their control. For his part, Richard Huntington wasn't a recent convert to Labour, having been a vocal supporter for some time—indeed, Saatchi & Saatchi had worked on Gordon Brown's 2010 campaign.

None of this stopped the headline carrying popular resonance. Labour shadow chancellor Rachel Reeves cited the article in her Autumn Statement response: "The ravens are leaving the tower when even Saatchi & Saatchi are saying the Tories aren't working."

For our purposes, what's interesting is the story the article tells. "The hardest task in marketing is to grow a declining category," writes Huntington. By his reading, democracy itself is a category in a decline: "People have always distrusted the motivations and character of politicians, but democracy rests on the belief that government itself can be an effective force for good in people's lives—and that is what is currently under threat." He goes on: "Regrettably, the idea of effective government has receded from the national consciousness."

There is a possible internal contradiction in the argument, in that it simultaneously blames a Conservative government's austerity politics for making life worse, while saying government has little power to change life in any direction. But it is true that general election voter turnout has declined, particularly among younger voters, despite a high turnout in the Brexit referendum. If that is down to a disenchantment with democratic politics, it's fair to wonder if it's connected to 15 years of purposeful advertising that offered consumption, not citizenship, as the answer to society's problems. If you can change the world by getting the right corporations on board, why bother with the slower work of campaigning and voting, especially when it can lead to outcomes you don't like?

With the chutzpah that is natural in the advertising world, Saatchi & Saatchi now offers to ride to the rescue of politics— by getting political parties to think more like an artisan gin: "To turn around a category that people are deserting in droves takes marketing superpowers," writes Huntington. "The most remarkable recent example is Sipsmith Gin, who defied the collapse of the global gin market to spur not only phenomenal growth for itself, but the revival of the whole category." Huntington admits this might be a strained comparison: "Sipsmith achieved this by restoring artisan copper-pot distilling to London, but in politics, it's easier said than done—especially with the lack of economic wiggle room available to any incoming government." True enough.

There are things to like in Huntington's analysis—he even writes about the importance of 'humility' when it comes to rebuilding connections with the public. But what's missing is a realisation of how the purpose narrative, in which adland is so deeply implicated, hovers behind this whole question. Having fuelled the delusion that the corporate sector can drive social change instead of politicians, the ad world now rides to the rescue of the political sector to teach them the lessons they've learned from reinventing the gin category.

The answer to an era of making brands sound like political movements is not an era of making political movements sound like brands. It's about reasserting the difference between the two. Ad agencies can play a role in multiple ways: returning to the core business of commercial creativity that works for real people, while putting their communication skills behind public sector and non-profit causes—not as side-interests, but as serious sectors that demand sustained commitment.

To do those jobs well, adland needs to rediscover two things. One is cognitive empathy. The other is creativity. The wider world could do with rediscovering them too.

Rediscovering cognitive empathy

"I'd like to describe a situation to you and have you develop a theory about what's going on in the mind of one of the people I describe. Here's the situation: A teacher asks the class a question and a student volunteers an answer and the teacher says, 'Well, I guess I've heard worse answers, but I can't remember when.' What do you think the student is feeling and/or thinking now?"[122]

In March 2023, Robert Wright, author of The Evolution of God, The Moral Animal and Nonzero, asked this question of ChatGPT-4, the large language model (LLM) that had recently been made available by OpenAI. The answer was impressive, picking up on the sarcastic intent of the teacher:

"Based on the situation you described, the student might feel embarrassed, disheartened, or upset due to the teacher's response, which seems to be critical and sarcastic. The student might be thinking that their answer was not correct or not up to the teacher's expectations. This experience could lead the student to feel hesitant about participating in future discussions or sharing their thoughts in class, fearing further negative feedback or judgment from the teacher."

ChatGPT-4 noted that this reaction might vary depending on the person: "While the provided scenario suggests a negative emotional response, it's possible that some individuals might react differently, focusing on improving their understanding or even finding humor in the situation." Asked to speculate on the response of other onlooking students in the class, ChatGPT-4 suggested that responses might range from sympathy to discomfort, amusement or indifference—all depending on the individuals and their relationships with the teacher and student in question.

Wright then asked a more complex question: What if there was a student who was romantically attracted to the current girlfriend of the student who had just been addressed sarcastically by the teacher? What would they be feeling?

ChatGPT-4 zeroed in on the most likely answer: "Schadenfreude: This student may feel a sense of satisfaction or pleasure from seeing the other student embarrassed, thinking that it might lower the other student's social standing or make the girlfriend reconsider their relationship." Other responses offered include "opportunism", "sympathy or empathy", "indifference" or "concern that the girlfriend might become upset or affected by the teacher's response to her boyfriend".

There's an interesting discussion to be had about how LLMs are able to generate such perceptive answers. The mechanic involves probabilistic predictions about which word comes next in the sentence, so it's all a highly sophisticated mimicry on one level. But you might also speculate about whether the LLM is effectively reverse-engineering a model of the human mind by looking at its linguistic output. Even the engineers aren't entirely sure what's going on inside.

All of that is for someone else's book. For the purposes of this section, our focus is on the skill that Robert Wright is asking ChatGPT-4 to demonstrate. It's known as 'cognitive empathy'. Not the emotional or affective empathy that involves sympathy or fellow feeling with the other person, but a more detached, non-judgmental attempt to take the perspective of somebody else, without endorsing it or sharing it yourself. Others call this 'perspective taking'. Either way, the point is that you don't have to *feel* schadenfreude to intuit that the romantic rival in this situation might be feeling it. You don't need to *approve* of them feeling schadenfreude. You don't necessarily need to be a young, heterosexual, conventionally schooled male, or to have had prior experience of being in that exact situation yourself, in order to exercise cognitive empathy effectively. You just need to cultivate the skill of understanding human nature and thinking yourself into the shoes of another person. No one can do it perfectly all the time, but life is difficult if we don't try to do it, at least some of the time.

It's particularly difficult if you work in advertising. The whole enterprise is meant to be about communicating effectively with particular audiences in particular contexts. In an earlier section on The Copy Book, we've seen how the best advertising copywriters do this: by focusing on the reader. What are they likely to be thinking? What questions are likely to be arising as they read? Why might they be sceptical? What's in this for them? That exercise involves a certain intellectual humility: realising how small a role your brand plays in someone's life (remember Coke and the 50% of buyers who barely ever think about it). It also involves realising how readers may be at least as smart, or smarter, than you are. As writer Tom Thomas says in The Copy Book: "If there's a simple truth that sums all this up—and there isn't but here goes anyway—it's that people who write ads should assume readers are at least as bright as they are. This has the advantage of being true some, maybe most, of the time. It also makes for honest writers—and credible ads."

Advertising people have historically assumed they're good at both cognitive and emotional empathy. Writers and designers feel they have an instinctive grasp of it. Ad agencies also employ planners and strategists whose role is to research audiences and markets and come up with broad insights that underpin each creative brief.

Particularly in recent years, the reality has been different. A 2019 white paper by strategy consultants Andrew Tenzer and Ian Murray brought some hard data to the question. In The Empathy Delusion, the authors used 14 psychological test questions to assess respondents on levels of cognitive empathy and emotional empathy. They found that ad people score about the same as everyone else (30% scoring highly, compared to 29% of non-advertising people). Not terrible, but also not great for one of the skills that advertising claims as a specialism.[123]

The same paper offers evidence that empathy is applied unequally: people on the left have a stronger tendency to judge their out-group more harshly, which is significant when 44% of advertising people self-identify as being on the left, compared to 25% of what the authors call the 'modern mainstream'—a generalist audience from all walks of life. So, as well as being no better at cognitive and emotional empathy than anyone else, ad people have a propensity to be worse, in the sense of over-identifying with one side and being less understanding of the other. One outcome of the purpose narrative is that ad agencies might even tout this as a strength rather than a weakness: they are proudly on the right side of history, and share their clients' bafflement or disdain when it comes to large swathes of the public.

In a more cognitively empathetic industry, ad agencies would take pride in being cultural listeners and interpreters. Whether you're a creative director or an account planner, if a client asks "What's going on in the minds of anti-vaxxers?" you should be ready with an answer. If another client asks "What's all this about the two-spirit community?" you should be ready to shed light. If a client is convinced Gen Z is demanding vocally left-wing marketing, you should be ready to explain why this isn't the case. You should take pride in being able to make good-faith arguments for Brexit or Trump, even if you don't agree with them. Equally, you should take pride in making the case for Just Stop Oil protests, even if you disagree with them.

To this end, you should cultivate a wide-ranging media diet, and continually seek to understand points of view that you don't share. Your agency should invest in rigorous, independent research rather than loose exercises with leading questions. And your agency recruitment should involve setting people briefs to advertise a cause or product with which they don't personally identify. Ask a 25-year-old to advertise a care home; ask a man to advertise sanitary towels; ask a Liverpool fan to work on an Everton merchandise campaign. (Incidentally, Everton's club shop in the 'Liverpool One' shopping centre is called 'Everton Two'—it's included in the latest edition of A Smile in the Mind, despite this co-editor being a Liverpool fan.)

None of this is to deny that people may gravitate towards causes they agree with, and some may have personal red lines, which is their right. But whatever your identity and outlook, it's impossible to build a career solely by marketing to people with exactly the same identity and outlook. At some point, everyone has to nurture the skill of cognitive empathy as best they can, because there is a big world out there.

Cognitive empathy has become unfashionable in the purpose era. Since the Occupy Wall Street protests receded and identity causes took over, it is seen as naive or problematic to suggest that you can transcend your own identity and connect with other audiences. Instead, diversity is pushed as the solution. If you want to market to diverse people, hire diverse people. Nothing about us without us. This is the cry, and there is some justification to it. Identity can be a shortcut to cognitive empathy: it's not unreasonable to think an agency made up of multiple ethnicities, sexual orientations, gender identities and class backgrounds will have better collective insight into mass-market audiences than an agency made up solely of privately educated straight white males.

But identity isn't a substitute for cognitive empathy. And over-emphasising it leads to unintended outcomes. It's a short step from 'We should hire a Muslim woman if we want to market credibly to Muslim women' to a workplace situation where everyone patronisingly turns to the one Muslim woman in the room and treats her as a spokesperson for her entire race, religion and gender. No one likes to feel reduced to their superficial identity traits, and the whole idea of representation veers close to that kind of identity determinism. It's a menstruation product, let's give it to the all-woman team. Actually, we'd quite like to work on the car ad, the women might reasonably reply. It's an urban youth brand, let's give it to the young black writer. Actually, I'm a Cambridge philosophy graduate and you're being weird, says the writer.

These aren't edge cases. A 2020 IPA industry survey found that 69% of Black and Asian Minority Ethnic (BAME) people in advertising were privately educated. This doesn't undermine the case for ethnic diversity, but it complicates it. A mix of class and educational backgrounds is relevant when it comes to mass marketing, but class is a hard thing to assess when recruiting. Do you go on self-identification, or do you ask intrusive personal questions about the applicant and the incomes of their parents and grandparents?

Another key variable is age. In the UK, spending by people aged 65 and over increased by 75% from 2001 to 2018, compared with a 16% fall in spending by those aged 50 and under during the same period. By 2040, it's predicted that older people will be responsible for 63p of every pound spent in the UK economy, up from 54p in 2018—and this will be spent across the economy, including recreation and culture, transport, and household goods and services.[124] Yet as the population ages, the ad industry is getting younger. The annual IPA survey suggests the average age of employees reduced marginally from 34.6 years in 2021 to 34.4 years in 2022, with only 6.5% of employees aged 50 or over.

A crude, demographically 'representative' approach would be to hire more old people. Indeed, it might even involve recruiting more old white men, given that 76.4% of the ad industry is white, compared to 82% of people in England and Wales; and 54.8% of adland is female, compared to 51% of the UK population. But it doesn't take long to see how clumsy and unpopular such an approach would be. And none of it takes into account other factors like the relative seniority and pay of these people, or traits like neurodiversity, disability, sexual orientation, political leaning, health challenges, or religious faith.

None of this is building up to saying let's forget the diversity conversation. But there is a case for raising it to a higher level. Right now, there's an understandable urge to build the 'business case' for diversity. But a stronger argument is that diversity is a moral good in its own right. Agencies should cast the net widely, be alert to their potential biases, and create a culture where people feel welcome long-term—because those are the right things to do. Indeed, in most cases, you'd be breaking the law to do otherwise. No other justification is needed, and as soon as you start making the 'business case', you get onto less solid ground.

Above all, diversity shouldn't be seen as a replacement for the hard work of cognitive empathy. However diverse your agency, it will achieve nothing without the key skill that every individual of every background needs to cultivate. Whoever you are, your job is to communicate with people who aren't you. That takes intellectual humility, imagination and a belief in the possibility of connection across divides. If that sounds daunting, it's also worth putting into perspective: in most real-world cases, the race, gender, religion, sexual orientation, class background and political persuasion of the audience aren't the most relevant variables. It's more: are they in the market for an electric car? Can they be persuaded to donate to this donkey shelter? Can we remind them Coke is the red swirly one when they buy a soft drink next year?

In all those cases, cognitive empathy can shape better answers, and help avoid some of the tone-deaf campaigns of recent years. And if ad agencies are reluctant to rediscover this core skill, there may soon be an alternative: we can get the machines to do it.

Reclaiming creativity

At a vacuum cleaner trade show in Lisbon in the mid-1970s, a bored founder and his sales rep were amusing themselves one evening by dressing up one of their machines in a ribbon and Union Jack badge, then drawing a crude smile under the vacuum hose connector, which began to look like a nose, followed by some eyes. They rolled the machine back to the corner with the other models, but the next day they noticed people were pointing and laughing. The founder, Chris Duncan, asked someone back at the office to design a proper face. With a nod to their British origins, they called it Henry. Four decades later, over 10 million Henry and Hetty hoovers have made their way to Downing Street, Buckingham Palace, and countless homes and offices around the world. Chris Duncan is worth over £150 million.

The addition of the face isn't purpose, or strategy, or positioning, or politics. It's creativity. Think of it as a distillation of the branding and marketing process: the job is to take an inanimate product or service and lend it a distinctive personality. It doesn't start with why. It starts with why not—a moment of unprofessionalism, messing about when you should be focusing on the goal of selling vacuum cleaners, not scribbling on them.

Why do people respond so well to it? Because we like anthropomorphic things. We like the playfulness of the smile, the levity it adds to everyday tasks. Amid the mundanity of labour, and the machinery of capitalism, Henry's smile is a mark that says we are human. And while it began with no social purpose, it found one in unexpected ways. Children love

Henry. In 2019, Erik Matich, a five-year-old with leukaemia, was flown from Illinois to Somerset by the Make-A-Wish charity, because it was his dream to see Henry's original home. Many children with autism have made a similar pilgrimage. "They seem to relate to Henry because he never tells them what to do," says Chris Duncan, who has subsequently worked with autism charities to create Henry and Hetty books.[125]

Visit Henry's website and you won't find a purpose statement. There is no "We are here to elevate the world's consciousness by humanising technology and delivering moments of transcendence to families and workers worldwide." The one moment the Henry brand wobbled was when the owner briefly expressed political views that could be interpreted as pro-Brexit.[126] Other than that, the brand has kept out of politics and strayed far from grandiosity or self-celebration. Its upmarket competitor Dyson has frequently appeared in design exhibitions and awards (until its owner began expressing pro-Brexit views of his own). But you won't find Henry celebrating himself in the same way. Others do it for him: in 2018, a Cardiff university student arranged a Henry hoover picnic and was forced to cancel it when 37,000 signed up to attend.[127]

Creativity is the ghost in the machine of capitalism. It's the spirit that takes an ordinary can of household oil, turns the spout into a beak, draws the rest of the bird on the can, then calls it Oily Bird to mimic the New Jersey accent of its owners. There's no record of who invented Oily Bird on behalf of the Ronson Corporation in 1964, but that person had a good day at the office, giving life to an enduring piece of commercial art.

Creativity is the spirit that wanders round an Audi factory in Germany, sees three words on a faded poster on the wall, and decides to use them as an ad slogan that no one in the UK will understand. 'Vorsprung durch Technik' became a popular catchphrase that evoked German engineering excellence, even though few people knew it meant 'Progress through technology'.[128]

Creativity is the spirit that wants to open a literacy and learning centre in downtown San Francisco, finds out that the location is reserved for retail use only, so decides to open a whimsical shop called the Pirate Supply Store, selling eye patches, skull flags and secret treasures. Sell those weird and wonderful things in the front, put the literacy centre in the back. That sidestep around the planning restriction became the inspiration for the Pirate Supply Store, Robot Supply Co, Brooklyn Superhero Supply Co, Hoxton Monster Supplies and other literacy centres around the world.

Only one of those ideas came from an ad person—it was John Hegarty of Bartle Bogle Hegarty who went wandering round the Audi factory floor. For that reason, it's common to hear people say 'Everyone is creative', arguing that creativity can't be hived off into a specialist department of an agency. But it's an incomplete truth. John Hegarty was also the only one who had to answer 50 other briefs that year. Everyone can be creative, just as everyone can dance. But some choose to do it professionally, returning to the blank page every day, with the pressure of filling it with something interesting and commercially viable.

There are competing methods of systematising creativity. James Kaufman and Ronald Beghetto have the 'four C'

THE ROAD TO HELL

model, which distinguishes mini-C (everyday play), little-C (everyday problem solving), pro-C (being professionally or vocationally creative) and big-C (creativity considered great in a certain field). The hierarchy implies a value judgment, but it's the distinctions themselves that are useful. In a meaningful sense, you're being creative every time you write an email, cook a meal, or create a PowerPoint slide. But collapsing all creativity down to one level, from the symphonies of Beethoven to the sending of a wink emoji, is losing some useful nuances.

In the context of advertising and branding, there is a point in the process when the schedule has been planned, the brief has been written, the fees have been agreed, the research is done, the strategy has been developed, and now there's a blank page where an ad, logo, slogan or idea needs to be. We can call what happens next writing, designing, crafting or ideating. We can make philosophical arguments about how nothing has been truly 'creative' since the Big Bang—it's all just riffing off what already exists. But the blank page still sits there, and 'creativity' is a pretty good word for what fills it, just as 'creatives' is a useful catch-all term for the art directors, designers and writers who do the work.

None of this is to talk down account management, media buying, research, strategy and planning, all of which serve an essential function and have a porous border with creativity. But most clients come to most agencies because they mostly need the creative part. They might need it to sell cars, raise funds, attract visitors, find job applicants, or inspire voters. The professional skill of creativity can be applied to all of those challenges, generating answers that range from the disarmingly obvious to the surprisingly lateral, all executed using the hard-earned craft skills of photographers, illustrators, directors and developers.

If you live and work outside the advertising and design industry, you might think I'm labouring an obvious point here. Yes, of course it's about the creative output and, for better or worse, agencies are the people who come up with it. But within the industry, creativity is talked about like an embarrassing old relative, who needs to be apologised for, or politely ignored.

"Creative excellence today means creativity that's not only great for the brief but for the world we're all part of," says the D&AD President, shielding the drunk uncle while he sings the WeBuyAnyCar jingle. "What creative excellence stood for 61 years ago is different from what we would celebrate as excellence today," says the D&AD Chief Executive as the uncle turns an oven glove into a handpuppet and sings 'Nothing's gonna stop us now'. "The nature of creativity has changed," shouts former WPP boss Martin Sorrell as the uncle yodels 'Domin-oh-hoo-hoo!' "Can we interest you in a campaign about suicide, or refugees?" says the Cannes Lions chairman as the uncle pours Pot Noodle into a pothole. "I'm an advert… and I just feel awful about it!" says the peaktime ad on Channel 4 while the uncle dons a gorilla costume and plays the drums.[129]

Ad agencies still come out with great, populist, commercially effective work. Much of it struggles to make the same impact it might have done in the 1970s or 1980s when the 'cultural commons' was broader. Back then, everyone was watching the same ad breaks at the same time on the same couple of channels, and talking about them in the workplace or school playground the next day. Now things are more fragmented, which drains advertising of some of its power, given that much of its effect comes not just from a personal response, but from the fact that we know everyone else is watching too.

Nevertheless, plenty of advertising still breaks through—sometimes through set-piece occasions like the Super Bowl in the US, or Christmas in the UK. But it also happens year-round, in ways so big that we barely notice them. It might be the Domino's yodel, or the McDonald's 'Raise your arches' campaign, turning an eyebrow gesture into a mimicking of the logo. Most of it doesn't carry the earnestness and supposed nobility of purposeful advertising, but it usually does a better job. In the UK, an agency called Brothers & Sisters churns out annoyingly effective ear worms for WeBuyAnyCar. But the agency is also a non-profit that funds great community work. You probably didn't know that because they don't go on about it.

Meanwhile, plenty of great design and branding takes place at multiple levels in society. For every bank or airline brand that makes some people shift uncomfortably, there is a branding scheme for a cancer research charity or a community farming organisation. Many agencies focus solely on that kind of work, either through ethical conviction or through a belief that there are more exciting creative opportunities, and it can make business sense to specialise.

Creativity oils the wheels of capitalism, some say. But it's too reductive to think that's all it does. Creativity can also jam a stick into the spokes of the wheel. It can subvert capitalism, find fun in it, seed ideas that challenge it. The State Street 'Fearless Girl' statue was a creative idea, but so was the Occupy Wall Street email. The Amazon logo is a creative intervention, but so is the indie bookshop with the charming shopfront. 'Labour isn't working' was a creative intervention for Margaret Thatcher, but so was 'Not flash, just Gordon' for Gordon Brown (both created by the same agency).

You would think advertising and design agencies would be keen to push this story widely. We exist to cultivate two skills: the cognitive empathy to help you understand the world, and the creativity to help you connect with it. To that end, we attract and employ people who think differently, are relentlessly curious about other points of view, come from a wide range of perspectives and backgrounds, and have this restless instinct to challenge received ideas.

If only it were so. Instead, the industry has been captured by a suffocatingly narrow political agenda, and a self-defeating distaste for its own successes. Industry leaders justify creativity with reference to social purpose. Industry awards place a narrow range of politically approved projects in the shop window, while the real work takes place elsewhere. Creative universities subjugate creativity to Chief Social Purpose Officers. Ad agencies run ads about how awful ads are.

The first step is to remake the commercial case for creativity: centre it, cultivate it, celebrate it. But it's also about more than that. Creativity can't be reduced solely to purpose, but it also can't be reduced solely to commerce. It can be its own justification. Henry's face sold more vacuum cleaners, but it also did something else. It spoke to a human need to create and connect, even while we live out our lives within the larger system of businesses and markets.

I don't mean this in a sentimental or quasi-spiritual way. It's as hard a fact as inflation or interest rates. Much branding and advertising work is created for a specific commercial purpose, which it fulfils but also transcends and outlasts. The elegant rejigging of the Friends logo into 'Ends Fri' was a specific answer to a specific brief in a specific week in 2004, but it endures as a piece of cultural history. Same with most of the jingles and ads you remember from childhood days, or many of the great logos that resonate in your brain in a way that signifies more than just a transport network (the London tube roundel) or a soft drink (the Coca-Cola swirly type) or a book company (Penguin).

Many come from little-known or sometimes entirely forgotten designers, art directors, writers and other 'creatives' who made the job better than it strictly needed to be. Yes, they did it for sound commercial reasons, but also for reasons of their own. There's an urge for human expression that goes beyond the corporate: an instinct to explore things for their own sake, and play around with ideas to see what happens.

Designer and illustrator Christophe Niemann once explained his process: "It's vital to keep experimenting. When I look at the backbone of what I do now, five years ago it was some weird, experimental thing that I was doing on a spare evening. Flip that thought around and you realise you will be stuck in five years' time if you aren't continuing to experiment now."[130]

I've tried to follow that advice over the years. Playing

around with downbeat twists on English proverbs led me to Perpetual Disappointments Diary, a demotivational journal that resonated in unexpected ways: I got a handwritten letter from one person, saying how it had consoled them after returning from their father's funeral. Being alone in a pub one day led me to write a topical poem and post it to Instagram—I kept doing it for three and a half years and it became one of the more meaningful projects in my life. Writing a Substack led me to make contact with a like mind in Australia, who ran the Antarctic Science Foundation, which led to a phone call, which led to a poetic manifesto that I wrote in 2023.

In 2017, I felt an urge to write a post about brand purpose for Creative Review magazine. Seven years later, I've emerged from a rabbit hole of marketing, philosophy, economics, politics and ethics to write this book.

None of it started with 'why'. But all of it can be seen as a perpetual search for it. If you're lucky, you find out your motivation somewhere towards the end of whatever it is you're doing. It comes from having an open mindset, not setting the goal in advance. Creativity ends with why.

In building this argument against corporate purpose, I've become more appreciative of how purpose matters at a human level: the yearning for it, the need for it. It's too big an idea to let corporations take it over. That's why I wrote this book.

Epilogue

OF COURSE, NOTHING WOULD have changed if I'd pressed delete.

Going back to that story in the prologue, I was witnessing an early instance of the 'purpose' word that was already on the rise and would go on to dominate the next decade and beyond.

2022 saw what could be the start of a purpose 'vibe shift'. Investor Terry Smith tore into Unilever's management for their uni-dimensional focus on purpose. Procter & Gamble's Mark Pritchard, a former purpose enthusiast, talked about the industry going 'too far into the good'.[131] Larry Fink mentioned the word only once in his 2023 letter. Alan Jope left Unilever and the new CEO has talked about purpose being an "unwelcome distraction". The Bud Light and Nigel Farage vs Coutts stories generated culture war heat, but also shed light on more serious arguments about the relationship of business and politics. Advertising awards even began to make noises about commercial creativity again.

But much of this is a change in tone rather than substance, and the deeper institutionalisation of purpose will be harder to dismantle. At Cannes, there has even been a move to introduce a new 'humour' category, supposedly as a way to acknowledge what was important all along, but in reality the final triumph of the cuckoo over the nest owner: purpose has taken over, now off you go to your specialist category.

More seriously, purpose continues to manifest in stories of political and corporate power, with the public in the firing line. In the UK, the Horizon scandal has engulfed the Post Office, whose Fujitsu-powered faulty software led to a series of accounting anomalies for which local sub-postmasters were relentlessly hounded, prosecuted and ground down by the system. Exposed in ITV drama Mr Bates vs the Post Office, this was a story of human beings fighting against the power of a brand whose reputation for trustworthiness was based on its bygone status as the General Post Office, but which in reality is now a façade placed over a quasi-privatised limited corporation under state ownership, and operating under severe commercial pressures. As usual, the circle is squared by the invocation of purpose: "An anchor of UK communities for centuries, Post Office is a commercial business driven by a strong social purpose" says their website. One of several villains in the tale is Paula Vennells, former CEO who is also an Anglican priest. As always, it's tempting to think these stories are down to bad actors with malevolent intentions. But the truth might be more disconcerting: what if the protagonists consider themselves decent people who are acting in service of a greater good, maybe to protect this vital, purposeful national asset? It's possible for anyone to lose their moral compass when money, power and status are involved, but purpose is the seductive narrative that makes it that much more likely.

Meanwhile, Thames Water has been on the brink of insolvency as water bills rise, environmental performance plummets, and the company struggles under the weight of £14 billion in debt, much of it due to historic mismanagement by the Australian Macquarie Group, whose profits continue to soar.[132] Then came a leaked email from Severn Trent

THE ROAD TO HELL

Water, whose CEO wrote to fellow water bosses to suggest pushing 'social purpose' as a strategic way to ward off nationalisation and keep their multimillion-pound pay and bonus packages. Liv Garfield wrote that this would involve "re-purposing utilities and utility networks into a new breed of declared social purpose companies—companies that remain privately owned, who absolutely can (and should) make a profit, but ones that also have a special duty to take a long-term view." For this, she claimed intellectual backing from Will Hutton, whose The State We're In never invoked the concept of 'purpose', but was an influential textbook for third-way stakeholder capitalism. Hutton subsequently wrote a supportive column in the Guardian.[133]

You could see a bright side in this. If 'social purpose company' becomes better established as a formal legal status, it may call the bluff of the companies who vaguely claim to be purpose-driven without adopting that status (as Thames Water has been doing for years). But the darker reality is that the formal status is itself a PR fudge lent the air of spurious legal authority. Maybe it's the final political backstop to the whole debate: an attempt to square the circle of private profit and public good in a way that makes the whole game of profit extraction that bit more subtle and well-mannered in future.

Over in the US, there has been a developing story about OpenAI as I've been writing this book. In a tangled tale of corporate power, involving the non-profit artificial intelligence research organisation and its for-profit subsidiary OpenAI Global, charismatic CEO Sam Altman was fired by his own board, then rapidly reinstated while much of the board resigned. The reasons for the dispute are contested, but fundamentally involve tensions between the non-profit mission of OpenAI and the for-profit incentives of its subsidiary—all of which have implications for the way this powerful technology develops. "The OpenAI meltdown shows that when nonprofits and for-profits clash, the one with the money usually wins," said Fortune magazine.[134] "OpenAI Is Now Unambiguously Profit-Driven, And That's A Good Thing," countered Forbes.[135] Whichever side you back, it's confirmation that the for-profit and not-for-profit divide is not a matter of semantics: it's a consequential distinction. Purpose is a PR move designed to elide the difference. It's a dry ice machine creating nice atmospherics without changing the underlying reality.

These ethical debates long preceded purpose, and will continue long after the word has receded. But they will become clearer and more honest if we turn off the dry ice machine and start to see the world as it is. If you're involved in the business and marketing worlds, please let your mental cursor hover over the word 'purpose' one last time. Then press delete.

Acknowledgements

Thanks to Sue, who has no doubt asked 'why' many times; Robin, who will do something better than this one day; David Pearson for lending his stellar cover design talent with such class and generosity; Sue again for pausing the painting and doing the typesetting; Jon Asbury for the editorial and fraternal advice; Miles and Rachel at Choir Press; Paul Feldwick, Michael Johnson, Andrew Kelly, Byron Sharp and Eliza Williams for reading and responding so generously; Patrick Burgoyne and Creative Review for publishing my early purpose writings; Robin Van Cleemput and all at Teamleader for inviting me to air these arguments for the first time in Ghent; Steve Harrison for the support I'll never publicly admit to receiving; Kate van der Borgh for the music; Mike Bryant, Justin Kirby, Rupert Newton, Tom Sharp and many others with whom I've had good conversations about all this; everyone who has subscribed on Substack or followed on social media; and Mum for the literary genes and literally everything else.

Cover design by David Pearson: typeasimage.com
Typesetting by Sue Asbury: sueasbury.co.uk

Notes

Introduction

1   'How much should arts unis be pushing purpose?' Creative Review, 4 April 2023

Chapter 1. What is purpose?

2   Sara Roberts and Jim Stengel quotes taken from 'Where Is Why Going?' Branding Roundtable 35, Branding Mag 2017

Chapter 2. Where did purpose come from?

3   'Shareholder value is no longer everything, Top CEOs say' New York Times, 19 August 2019

4   'Growth and Quality of Life' Keynote speech given by M. Antoine Riboud, 25 October 1972

5   'Danone adopts new legal status to reflect social mission' Financial Times, 26 June 2020

6   'Danone: A case study in the pitfalls of purpose' Financial Times, 18 March 2021

7   From Savage Minds podcast interview, 28 March 2010

8   'Many fairy tales about the brain still propagate through our field' Interview with British Psychological Society, 31 January 2017

9   'Story of Wright brothers' work continues to enthrall Tise' Interview with East Carolina University, 13 October 2009

10   Savage Minds podcast interview, 28 March 2010

11   'The flawed Stengel Study of Business Growth' Byron Sharp, 30 December 2011

12   'Why was Jim Stengel's 'Grow' so popular when it's so flawed?' Richard Shotton, 11 November 2015. Also see his book The Choice Factory.

13   "'Arrogance' around brand purpose making consumers distrust ads'

Marketing Week, 29 June 2017

Chapter 3. How purpose leads to bad marketing

14   'Is this the end for brand purpose?' Creative Review, 19 June 2017
15   The brands in order are Airbnb, WeWork, Uber, Facebook, Starbucks and Spotify
16   'Repeats Suggestion That We Buy Belgium, John Wanamaker in Earnest' New York Times, 24 July 1915
17   Incidentally, many users of that meme forget that the point of the scene was that Don Draper had indeed been thinking about that guy for the preceding 24 hours. But this is not helpful for making my point.
18   "True Gen': Generation Z and its implications for companies' McKinsey, 12 November 2018
19   'Understanding Generation Z in the workplace' deloitte.com
20   'New research shows consumers more interested in brands' values than ever' Consumer Goods Technology Magazine, 27 April 2022
21   PC Consumer Intelligence Series, 2 June 2021
22   'From Amazon to Skittles, a new survey of the top 20 brands among Gen Z adults shows tech and snack brands reign supreme with the demographic' Business Insider, 2 October 2022
23   'Meet the Gen Z brand whisperers' The Guardian, 22 April 2023
24   "Post-truth' climate impacts Gen Z's conflicting brand perceptions, Forrester says' 20 January 2021
25   'IPA research reveals consumer support of brand response to Ukraine invasion' Not-entirely-accurately-headlined article on ipa. co.uk, 31 March 2022
26   'Cross-Tabs: October 2023 Times/Siena Poll of the 2024 Battlegrounds' New York Times, 5 November 2023
27   'Poll: Biden's standing hits new lows amid Israel-Hamas war' NBC, 19 November 2023
28   '90 years of doing good – why companies with purpose last' Unilever, 13 January 2020
29   'Mayonnaise with 'purpose' rebuke shows discontent Unilever is

facing' Financial Times, 12 January 2022

30 'Lip Gloss, Potato Chips, Air Fresheners Are Among the
    'Essentials' Still Sold in Russia' Wall Street Journal, 22 March 2022

31 'Danone chief defends staying open for business in Russia' The
    Times, 9 March 2022

32 'Danone CEO directs brands to be bold or die' Sustainable Brands,
    2019

33 'Unilever's new chief says corporate purpose can be 'unwelcome
    distraction'' Financial Times, 26 October 2023

34 'The effectiveness of Brand Purpose' Peter Field, IPA EffWorks
    Global 2021

35 'The Meltdown of a Gay Bank' New Yorker Intelligencer, 31 March
    2023

36 'Gen Z want to work 'lazy girl jobs'. Who can blame them?' The
    Guardian, 9 July 2023

37 'Quiet quitting: why doing the bare minimum at work has gone
    global' The Guardian, 6 August 2022

38 'State of the Global Workplace: 2023 Report' Gallup

39 'Ian Leslie: Does Brand Purpose Have a Point?' APG Noisy
    Thinking, 21 September 2017

Chapter 4. How purpose leads to a worse world

40 'Severn Trent chief proposes 'social purpose' water firms amid
    utilities crisis' The Guardian, 30 June 2023; and 'NatWest poised to
    report biggest profits since 2008 financial crisis' The Guardian, 12
    February 2023

41 'Should firms increase advertising expenditures during recessions?'
    KD Frankenberger and RC Graham, 2003

42 'Moldy Whopper' D&AD Awards 2020

43 Sourced from Johan Norberg's The Capitalist Manifesto, p.233

44 'Would you choose a Costa coffin to meet your maker?' The
    Guardian, 18 February 2014

45 Most of these two paragraphs are taken from my first article about
    purpose, published in Creative Review, June 2017

46 "Consumers are lost forever': Bud Light sales remain 30% down since Dylan Mulvaney marketing debacle six months ago' Daily Mail, 9 September 2023

47 'Why California Rejected Racial Preferences, Again' The Atlantic, 10 November 2020

48 'A Campaign to Remind Us That We Love New York (City)' New York Times, 23 March 2023

49 'The We Heart NYC logo flop' New Yorker, 23 March 2023

50 'These New Yorkers don't heart the We Heart NYC logo' New York Times, 21 March 2023

51 'New Yorkers bond over new city logo: They hate it' Washington Post, 21 March 2023

52 From the film Midnight Cowboy (1969). The scene was apparently improvised by Hoffman and involved a real and perfectly oblivious cab driver.

53 'Juror from Elizabeth Holmes trial says it was tough to convict the former Theranos CEO' Business Insider, 5 January 2022

54 'WeWork: they've transformed the office, now it's time for your home' The Guardian, 11 January 2016

55 'I was Zuckerberg's speechwriter. "Companies over countries" was his early motto.' Kate Losse, Vox, 16 April 2018

56 @doctorow Twitter thread, 10 August 2021

57 'The IPA Effectiveness Awards are not 'watering down their criteria'' Campaign, 17 February 2022

58 'Cadbury's US owners paid ZERO corporation tax in UK despite profits rocketing by more than 700 per cent to £185million' Daily Mail, 11 October 2018

59 'Cadbury's non-payment of tax on UK profits' Early Day Motion 832, tabled 8 December 2016

60 'Cadbury owner paid no UK corporation tax last year' The Guardian, 6 December 2015

61 'Cadbury: the great tax fudge' Financial Times, 20 June 2013

62 "Brands to avoid': Mars and Cadbury among chocolate firms criticised in ethics report' The Observer, 2 December 2023

NOTES

63 'IPA reacts to appointment of new Prime Minister Liz Truss' ipda. co.uk 5 September 2022

64 'Marketers, like chancellors, need time in the job to succeed' Marketing Week, 20 October 2022

65 'Good for nothing' nickasbury.substack.com 18 November 2022

66 'Brands take note: The purpose of purpose is purpose' Marketing Week, 16 September 2022

67 'Marketers, like chancellors, need time in the job to succeed' Marketing Week, 20 October 2022

68 'Charities need to remember why they exist – and shout about it' The Guardian, 6 April 2016

69 'As companies become purpose-led, where does that leave charities?' Fast Company, 15 August 2018

70 'Why charity brands now need brand purpose' The Team, 16 October 2019

71 'Heinz switches slogan to 'Beanz Meanz More' as part of purpose drive' Marketing Week, 20 September 2021

72 'Creativity is purpose enough' nickasbury.substack.com 29 June 2022

73 'James Purnell: Designing a university around social purpose – one year in' UAL LinkedIn article, 15 March 2022

74 Creative Industries report, great.gov.uk

75 'BlackRock Closes In on the Once Unthinkable, $10 Trillion in Assets' Wall Street Journal, 14 July 2021

76 'Nudging out support for a carbon tax' David Hagmann, Emily H. Ho, George Loewenstein, 1 June 2019

77 'Fink: 'Capitalists Should Self-Regulate' on Climate Disclosure' Bloomberg Television, 27 January 2021

78 'Tariq Fancy on Stuart Kirk, the Republicans and what's next for ESG' Financial Times, 20 June 2022

79 'Corporate Sustainability: First Evidence on Materiality' Khan, Serafeim and Yoon, November 2016

80 'Corporate Sustainability: A Model Uncertainty Analysis of Materiality' Berchicci and King, January 2022

81 'Honey, I Shrunk the ESG Alpha' Scientific Beta, April 2021

82 'The game of ESG telephone' GreenBiz, 10 August 2022

83 'ESG outperformance narrative 'is flawed', new research shows' Financial Times, 3 May 2021

84 'Bulb Energy bailout to cost UK taxpayers £6.5bn' Financial Times, 17 November 2022

85 ASA Ruling on Innocent Ltd, 23 February 2022

86 'The Guardian view on festive marketing: stop spending like there's no tomorrow' The Guardian, 21 November 2023

87 'Ad industry grapples with role selling consumption in climate crisis' The Guardian, 21 November 2023. Citing 'Ecoffectiveness: The Missing Measure in a Climate Crisis' The Great Reset, 2018

88 'Ad chiefs warn: 'Advertised emissions won't help our industry to reach net zero'' Campaign, 15 June 2023

89 'Ad industry grapples with role selling consumption in climate crisis' The Guardian, 21 November 2023

90 'The Real Truth About Beauty: A Global Report – Findings of the Global Study on Women, Beauty and Well-Being' September 2004

91 'Dove's beauty campaign 'has turned on the women it claims to champion'' Globe and Mail, 9 April 2015

92 'Sorry Dove, empowerment isn't a personal care product' The Guardian, 9 April 2015

93 'The Effectiveness of the Dove Campaign for Real Beauty in Terms of Society and the Brand' Lindsey Morel, 1 May 2009

94 'The Truth About Beauty' The Atlantic, March 2007

95 'Dove's 'Real Beauty' pics could be big phonies' AdAge, 7 May 2008

96 'Beauty Above All Else: The Problem With Dove's New Viral Ad' The Cut, 18 April 2013

97 Top 15 Ad Campaigns of the 21st Century, AdAge, 12 January 2015

98 'Mark Ritson on how Dove challenged beauty industry stereotypes' Marketing Week YouTube channel, 2019

99 'Stop the Scroll: The secrets to creating distinctive TikTok ads that entertain and deliver' Kantar, 30 March 2023

NOTES

100 'Is this the end for brand purpose?' Creative Review, 19 June 2017

101 '4 great lessons on confidence from Mindy Kaling' Vox, 7 August 2015

102 'Unilever injects extra £442m into marketing amid 'digital hubs' investment' Marketing Week, 9 February 2023

103 'Statistics about women and girls' mental health' Mental Health Foundation 2017 report

104 'Unilever Will Drop the Word 'Fair' From its Skin-Lightening Creams' Time, 26 June 2020

105 'Nice profit margins, Unilever, but spare us the 'sharing the pain' gloss' The Guardian, 25 July 2023

106 'Unilever named 'international sponsor of war' by Ukraine' The Guardian, 3 July 2023

Chapter 5. What's the alternative?

107 blog.yorksj.ac.uk/jovannalleshi/patagonia-sustainability

108 'Yvon Chouinard And The Patagonia Purpose Trust— What Is It And Will It Work?' Forbes, 16 September 2022

109 'An Unusual $1.6 Billion Donation Bolsters Conservatives' New York Times, 22 August 2022

110 'Patagonia's radical business move is great – but governments, not billionaires, should be saving the planet' The Guardian, 20 September 2022

111 Dick Ponte, quoted in Shameless Exploitation in Pursuit of the Common Good

112 'The Newman's Own Exception' Collier Law blog post, 12 February 2020

113 'From Rabbie to Rubens: 10 years of free entry to museums' The Guardian, 30 November 2011

114 'Who's laughing now? Let's stop the decline of humor in advertising' Kantar, 3 February 2022

115 'Left-Handed Mango Chutney' Zulu Alpha Kilo YouTube channel

116 'About Advertising: Bernbach Puts Agency's Iron Fist in Velvet Glove' Los Angeles Times, 11 January 1971

117 'Doyle Dane Cigaret Ban Ended' New York Times, 20 December 1982

118 'Geoffrey Chaucer note asking for time off work identified as his handwriting' The Guardian, 10 July 2023

119 'A Life in the Day of a window cleaner at the World Trade Center, 1998' Sunday Times, 4 January 1998. I came across the quote via Joe Moran, in a blog post dated 20 April 2011 at joemoransblog.blogspot.com

120 'Thatcher ad chief: We don't want five more years of cruelty with the Tories' The Independent, 24 November 2023

121 'A rare outing for a defiant Maggie: Baroness Thatcher attends Saatchi's 40th anniversary party' Daily Mail, 10 September 2010

122 'ChatGPT is capable of cognitive empathy!' nonzero.substack.com 30 March 2023

123 'The Empathy Delusion' Andrew Tenzer and Ian Murray, Reach Solutions 2018

124 'UK retirees' spending rockets as younger people spend less' The Guardian, 2 January 2020

125 'Sucks to be him! How Henry the vacuum cleaner became an accidental design icon' The Guardian, 24 July 2021

126 'Investment supports Henry manufacturer growth' Stephen Farrell, Insider Media, 19 September 2016

127 'Man arranged picnic to celebrate Henry the Hoover and 37,000 people wanted to go' Metro, 10 March 2018

128 'Vorsprung durch Technik – ad slogan that changed how we saw Germany' The Guardian, 18 September 2012

129 First quote from Naresh Ramchandani, D&AD President, 2021. Second quote from Jo Jackson, CEO of D&AD (2023). The oven gloves ad was by Morrison's and Leo Burnett (2023).

130 From an interview in A Smile in the Mind (Phaidon, 2016)

Epilogue
131 'P&G's Marc Pritchard: 'the industry has gone too far with purpose marketing'' The Drum, 17 June 2022

132 'As Thames Water sinks, Macquarie Group continues its unstoppable rise' The Guardian, 10 July 2023

133 'Water boss Garfield's email to rivals is more collusion than good deed' Evening Standard, 30 June 2023; and 'Now, water bosses, you must show how capitalism can work for the common good' The Guardian, 2 July 2023

134 'The OpenAI meltdown shows that when nonprofits and for-profits clash, the one with the money usually wins' Fortune, 21 November 2023

135 'OpenAI Is Now Unambiguously Profit-Driven, And That's A Good Thing' Forbes, 9 December 2023

Index

Biography

Nick Asbury is a creative writer who has worked in branding, strategy and design for 25 years. As a commentator, creative writer and experimental poet, he has written for Creative Review, Design Week and The Guardian and been profiled in the New York Times, Irish Times and Sydney Morning Herald. Nick is featured in The Copy Book: How Some of the World's Best Advertising Writers Write Their Advertising (Taschen) and co-authored A Smile in the Mind: Witty Thinking in Graphic Design (Phaidon). Other works include humorous journal Perpetual Disappointments Diary (Pan Macmillan), three-year poetry project Realtime Notes, described by critic John Self as 'the best chronicle of the 21st century', and ongoing adventures in Tin Pan Alley-style songwriting at songwritings.substack.com Since writing about purpose for Creative Review in 2017, Nick has been a frequent commentator on the ethics and politics of advertising, mainly through his Substack 'Thoughts on Writing' at nickasbury.substack.com

Follow and connect at:
nickasbury.com
nickasbury.substack.com
x.com/asburyandasbury
or find me on LinkedIn

Milton Keynes UK
Ingram Content Group UK Ltd.
UKHW010901080524
442402UK00004B/133